Contents

Acknowledgements

I have a theory that this world of ours would be much improved if it were governed by those people who grow plants and tend gardens. They have characteristics which could be invaluable to mankind, and their virtues – especially during the latter part of the twentieth century – are refreshing and increasingly rare. I am not suggesting the stereotypic traits of patience and dependability, though they are implicit, but rather the old-fashioned values which gardeners embrace.

Our present world is selfish, pessimistic and negative but the plantsmen whom I have met during the preparation of this book have been entirely helpful and courteous. I could offer them nothing, but they willingly gave me the most valuable of all gifts – their time.

My grateful thanks to Tony Byers of Suttons Seeds; Andrew Unwin; Paul Hansord and David Batty of Thompson and Morgan; Mr McLean of Brown and Co; Paul Griffiths of Harlow Car Gardens; John Whitehead of Colegrave Seeds; Brian Crosby of the British Bedding Plant Association; Mr Don Williams of Sheffield Botanic Garden; and Peter Atkinson of Springfields Gardens.

Special thanks are due to Stuart Coutts of Four Oaks Nursery whose impatiens I have been trying for years and to Harry Anderton whose advice and friendship I value greatly.

For every silver lining there must be a cloud and in my case, the shadows have been cast by Kathy, Robin, Chris and Nick . . . but their encouragement has been ever present.

BEDDING
PLANTS

■ Step by Step to Growing Success ■

Ian Murray

CROWOOD GARDENING GUIDES

First published in 1991 by
The Crowood Press Ltd
Gipsy Lane
Swindon
Wiltshire
SN2 6DQ

British Library Cataloguing in Publication Data

Murray, Ian
  Bedding plants.
  1. Great Britain. Bedding plants. Cultivation
  I. Title
  635.9620941

ISBN 1 85223 353 2

Other titles available in this series:
Bonsai, Indoor Bonsai, Garden Design, Conservatory Gardening, Fuchsias,
Container Gardening, Cacti and Succulents, Pelargoniums, Clematis, Water
Gardens, Climbing Plants and Wall Shrubs, and Organic Gardening

Picture Credits
Photographs by Ian Murray
Line illustrations by Claire Upsdale-Jones

Typeset by Avonset, Midsomer Norton, Bath
Printed and bound by Times Offset Pte. Ltd, Singapore

Introduction

Of all the particular areas of gardening, perhaps bedding is the most difficult to define but fortunately most gardeners appreciate what is meant by the term and others will find the distinctions academic and spurious. Many of the plants described in this book are more famous in other roles, as pot subjects for the home or greenhouse, but their use in the garden also earns them the title of bedding plants. If separate categories are required for descriptive purposes, then I would suggest that it is the way in which a plant is used which should determine the appropriate designation.

The essential characteristic of bedding is its temporary nature and its ability to complement the more permanent features of the garden, in either a subtle or a dramatic way. Schemes can be changed annually or seasonally and with comparative ease, allowing the designer to respond to the transient dictates of fashion or the fluctuations of personal preference. For artistic gardeners, the trowel becomes the paintbrush; beds and borders are the canvas and the use of colour and form is only limited by the imagination.

For some years now, the trend has been for using colour in its more intense forms but the indicators are now pointing towards pastel shades and a more discreet use of the spectrum. However, there is no reason why the grand perceptions of garden displays should influence the individual. We all know where beauty lies and in this case the beholder should exercise the right to determine every component of the overall scene.

Current concerns about the environment have applied gentle pressure on gardeners to embrace the natural look by letting the lawn grow as it will and by making random sowings of wild flowers. The inference is that the cultivation of sub-tropical species is somehow anathema to the spirit of ecological balance and against the interests of wildlife. This is nonsense and nobody should feel guilty about a preference for plants which originate in foreign lands. In the pure sense of the word, modern gardens are not natural but they satisfy the human quest for beauty and they remain oases of sustenance and protection for a wide variety of fauna.

Gardeners, by definition, are concerned about living things and their aspirations to beautify the surroundings make them positive contributors towards improving a planet which is otherwise on the decline. However, I have no desire to elevate bedding plants into the realms of philosophy but rather to endorse their value and commend them to gardeners everywhere. They give delight and joy and enable us to create a pleasureable landscape in which to live, at little cost or effort and with infinite variety.

CHAPTER 1

To Sow or not to Sow?

That is the question which must be answered at some point but it has nothing to do with the nobility of the gardener's mind; it is merely a matter of personal preference or convenience. For some, the process of deciding what seed to buy and from where, coupled with the extra responsibility of cultivating plants from scratch, is irksome in the extreme. Much more appealing is the prospect of responding to impetuosity on the day of planting by popping down to the garden centre and buying a ready-made display. For busy people and those who anticipate few pleasures from sowing seed, there is much to be said for instant bedding but there are other options which enable you to buy partly developed plants.

Seedlings can be purchased, thus by-passing the primary stage of producing bedding plants, and so-called 'plugs' are available which also remove the chore of pricking out and although the plants are more expensive at each successive stage, the economics of bedding are not just a matter of comparing prices. Mature plants require no equipment apart from a trowel, and seedlings and plugs do away with the necessity for germination equipment but need to be grown under protection. Clearly, the cost of a packet of seed which may produce dozens or even hundreds of plants is considerably lower than buying the same number of mature or partly developed subjects. However, the consequent cost of heating a greenhouse solely for bedding plants would not be economic – unless it were for very large numbers. If the greenhouse is heated (at least partly) for other purposes or if plants are raised in the home, then the situation is quite different. Now that you have been warned about the negative points of raising from seed, it must be said that it can be the most absorbing part of horticulture.

STARTING FROM SEED

Whether it is the familiar coconut, some of which weigh over 40lb (18kg) or the dust-like seed of begonias at more than two million to the ounce (100,000 per gram), these embryonic plants are quite miraculous. The organic material in a coconut is very evident but what about the minute and apparently inert capsules which characterize the seeds of many species? Each seed contains all the information and 'stuff' which

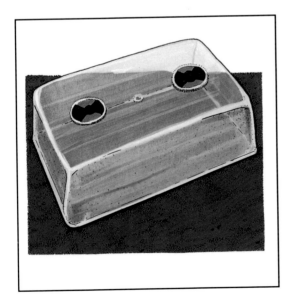

Fig 1 A propagator top used as a cloche.

enable it to grow into an organism recognisably similar to its parents and enables the species to survive conditions which are not favourable to the plants themselves. Seeds are produced from sexual reproduction and this ensures the inheritance of specific characteristics in subsequent generations – and also allows the possibility of slight changes over long periods of time.

The main drawback to growing from seed is that a certain amount of equipment is desirable and, ideally, a greenhouse or conservatory is needed so that a start can be made when outside conditions are unfavourable. That is not to say that an enthusiast cannot make do with window-sills but every packet of seed should carry a warning! A packet of petunia seed, for instance, may be sown in a half-tray measuring 8×4in (20×10cm) but even with only partial success, a hundred seedlings at least will result. These will need pricking out so that they have adequate space for growth and this means that they will require eight or ten times the original area. All too soon, this expansion will take over all the window-sills in the house and although some dedicated households may take it in their stride, others may not be so tolerant.

Hygiene

A prerequisite for success with seeds is a fairly strict amount of cleanliness and this involves disinfecting seed trays, pots and the propagator with a mild, household disinfectant. This is not to demonstrate the fastidiousness of gardeners but rather to ensure that pests and disease organisms are not given the opportunity to proliferate. The high temperatures needed for the germination of many seeds provide a suitable environment for many undesirables.

It is also essential, in my view, to use a sterilized compost which will satisfy the hygiene requirements and also ensure that there will be few, if any, weed seeds to take advantage of perfect growing conditions. Of course, it is possible to use garden soil, but diseases are often present there and weeds will certainly ensue, all at

the expense of your cherished seedlings. Ideally, a specific seed compost should be used because the germination of some seeds and the subsequent growth of the seedlings can be inhibited by the chemical nutrients which are part of the formula for potting composts.

Another source of possible contamination – and one which is often overlooked – is watering equipment and indeed the water itself. Many greenhouse owners use rain-water collected in butts and tanks and this allows the introduction of a large variety of pathogens. One of the most common problems is the growth of algae over the compost surface and this can often be traced to rain-water storage. A film of algae will invariably be found in watering cans and this should be removed before the seed-sowing season arrives. Permanganate of potash crystals were widely used by older generation gardeners but these are not so available nowadays; instead, there are many modern sterilants and disinfectants which you can use. However, even if you take every possible precaution, it is probably more prudent to use tap water for germination and the early stages of plant growth.

Containers for Sowing

The choice of receptacle used for sowing seed is largely a matter of personal choice and the plastic age has given us a wide variety of alternatives. Traditionally, a shallow seed tray has been used but this has no distinct advantage over pots or margarine tubs. The important decision is about the ideal size for your purposes and if you require a couple of 100 seedlings of a small variety, then the half-tray or its equivalent plastic container will suffice. If, however, the same number of large seedlings are needed, then the full tray – 14×8in (35×20cm) – should be used. If you have not grown from seed before, the simple rule is that large seeds beget large seedlings. Where only small numbers of plants are raised, small plant pots or kitchen containers will be ideal, but remember with the latter that holes must be made in the base to allow for drainage.

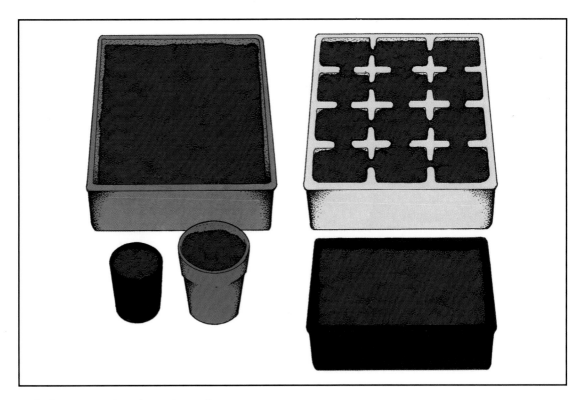

Fig 2   Suitable containers for sowing seeds.

Fig 3   Sowing equipment – heated and unheated propagators, containers and a thermometer.

Compost

Peat-based composts are the norm these days, and the soil-based mixtures are more difficult and more expensive to obtain but both will do the job admirably. Seed needs air, moisture and the appropriate temperature for germination; the compost facilitates the first two, whilst we arrange for the heat. The compost should fill the container to within about ½in (lcm) from the top and it should then be gently, very gently, firmed. Undue pressure will compact the medium and inhibit the growth of shoots and roots; it may also exclude the necessary air, so rely on the watering process to settle the compost. For the first watering, I believe that Cheshunt compound should be added as a deterrent to fungus problems such as 'damping off'. Cheshunt is merely a mixture of two common chemicals, copper sulphate and ammonium carbonate, at the rate of loz (about 30g) to 2gal (9l) of water. As with all garden chemicals, care is needed in their use and it is important to read the instructions carefully. With Cheshunt compound, you will notice a slight smell of ammonia but this is quite normal.

Large Seed

When the container and compost preparation is complete, large seed can be sprinkled directly from the packet or if the seeds are large enough, they can be individually placed on the surface with about ½in (lcm) space between them. This spacing is important because it prevents the roots from intermingling at an early stage and makes pricking out much simpler. When you are satisfied with the even spacing of the seeds, they should be covered by about ¼in (½cm) of compost and watered gently.

Small Seed

Begonias are perhaps the best example but they are also the worst to sow. (They come in the shape of dust-like particles which are awkward to disperse and often difficult to even see.) Firstly, you should tap the packet sharply to ensure that all the seed falls to the bottom, and then carefully open the top. When it comes to sprinkling the seed over the compost, this must be done in good light because you will only be able to see the seed as it leaves the packet, not as it lands. There is a body of opinion which advocates mixing fine seed with sand to enable effective distribution but it can add to the complications. Whatever you try, the results are likely to be patchy; consequently, the seeds will be in clusters

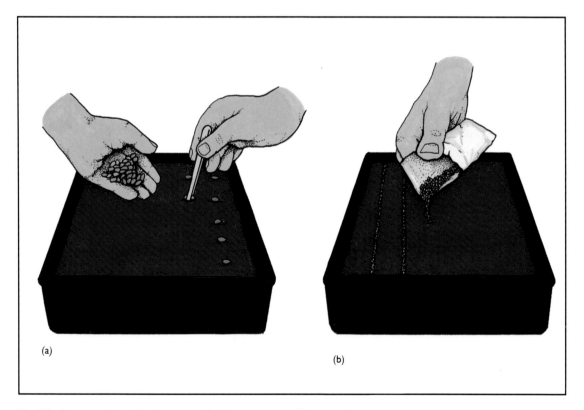

(a)

(b)

Fig 4(a) Large seeds can be 'space sown' using tweezers or fingers and thumbs.
   (b) Fine seeds can be gently tapped from the packet.

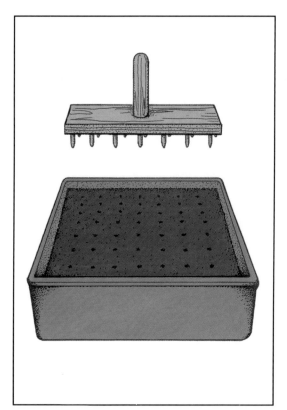

Fig 5   A dibalot is ideal for firming the
compost, marking out spacing for pricking out
and sowing large seeds.

Fig 6   With plants such as geraniums which
bear large seed, it is a simple matter to ensure
that they are sown with ample space between
them.

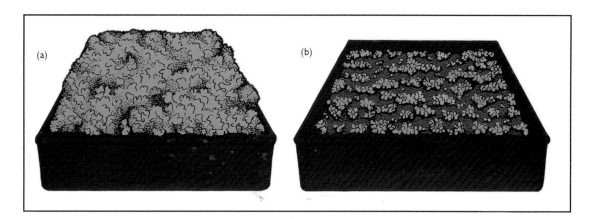

Fig 7(a)   Seedlings from thickly-sown seeds.
    (b)   Seedlings from sparsely-sown seeds.

and pricking out will be more difficult but not too much so. Perhaps I should also mention that coughs and sneezes during this fine-seed operation are disastrous and will result in some financial loss — the seed of some begonias carries a wholesale price above £5,000 per oz (30g).

The other vital consideration with fine seed is that it should not be covered with compost but only carefully watered, or preferably sprayed, so that the seeds are settled in position. Some fine seed also needs to be kept in the light for optimum germination and this information is listed in the Sowing Tables, page 123.

GERMINATION

Having recognised the main requirements of successful germination as being moisture and a fairly high temperature, it is simple to identify a propagator as the most effective and economical means of achieving this. However, the capital cost of the thermostatically controlled models is such that only enthusiasts are likely to make the investment, although a propagator is also excellent for rooting cuttings. In the absence of such equipment, you must improvise by building your own simple structure, using wood, transparent plastic and perhaps a soil-heating cable (but even this may be too elaborate for modest propagation needs). If the seed tray is enclosed in a plastic bag and kept in a warm place, accurate control of conditions may be impossible, but nevertheless, good results are possible. If the home must serve as the germination area, then the airing cupboard is undoubtedly an excellent source of fairly steady warmth but as it is dark, some seeds will not germinate well. However, a dark position is suitable for most subjects and the only danger is in leaving them in the dark after emergence has taken place. Regular inspection is essential and as soon as the first shoots are seen, the tray must be put in a light and warm spot.

Once germination has taken place, the seedlings will need coddling for a week or so and should then be gradually accustomed to the

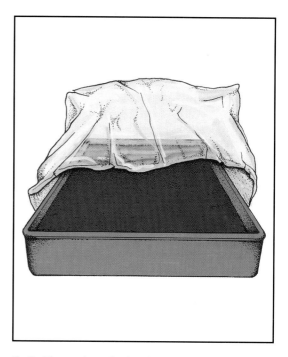

Fig 8   The seed tray is placed in a plastic bag to maintain humidity.

Fig 9   Young geraniums a few weeks after germination need maximum light for sturdy growth and a minimum temperature of 50°F (10°C).

lower temperatures which will prevail during the next stage. After the week in intensive care, the plastic bag should be removed to let the young plants benefit from good air circulation – but without draughts. If the compost shows signs of drying out, then watering should take place, again using a solution of Cheshunt compound.

PRICKING OUT

This is a task which requires a combination of concentration and manipulative skills. Patience and care are essential to avoid damage and it is one of those jobs which can only be learned by experience.

As soon as the seedlings are large enough to handle, they should be pricked out and, even with very small plantlets, it is better to do the job earlier rather than later. Plants which are growing close together have an annoying habit of entwining their roots and the process of separating

them can be tedious. This is particularly true of begonias and impatiens which have rather fragile connections between stems and roots, and careless handling will lead to damage that only becomes apparent later.

Hold the seedlings only by the leaves with the finger and thumb of one hand, while with the other you use a small stick to lever the roots out of the compost. If more than one seedling comes out, separate them carefully, again using the leaves to hold them, and although it is sometimes recommended that lobelia and other tiny subjects should be pricked out in small clumps, I believe that individual treatment is better. This is especially so where mixed seed is being grown, otherwise the result will be different-coloured flowers on what appears to be one plant.

When the single plantlet has been safely extracted, make a hole in the new compost with the stick so that the roots can be accommodated without undue cramping. Push the compost over the roots and up to the base of the leaves; no

Fig 10 Pricking out seedlings.

Fig II *Large seedlings such as geraniums can be pricked out into pots.*

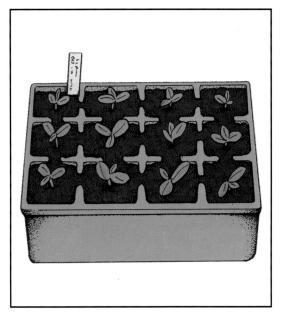

Fig I2 *Newly pricked out seedlings in stagger pots.*

pressure is needed because the seedlings will be adequately firmed by the subsequent watering.

Potting compost is the best medium for pricking out and I also think that stagger pots or other unit containers should be used because all plants will be more vigorous in the absence of competition and bedding out becomes a much easier task. Otherwise, use trays or boxes which are at least 2in (5cm) deep and space the plants to allow for future growth. Expensive and larger subjects, such as geraniums, are better put into 3½in (9cm) pots on their own.

GROWING ON

Maximum light is essential for sturdy development but the seedlings should not be subjected to direct sunshine until about a week after pricking out and, if possible, a minimum temperature of 50°F (10°C) should be maintained. Watering can be critical with some subjects and in general it is desirable to grow on the dry side, never

allowing the compost to become really wet. This is very important if you are unable to provide reasonably warm conditions.

Window-sills are not perfect for the growing on stage because however bright the window seems to be, it will receive far less light than in an outdoor position or in a greenhouse. The 'one-sided' light also means that containers must be turned around, at least every other day, to avoid the plants being drawn in one direction. Impatiens, begonias and many other bedding plants can grow quite successfully next to house windows but geraniums, which prefer high light intensity, will often become rather spindly specimens.

In the greenhouse, the problem is that growing-on temperatures are expensive to provide during the early part of the year. There are cheaper alternatives, however: a glass or clear plastic structure can be used within the greenhouse, preferably close to the heat source, or part of the greenhouse can be partitioned using a simple drape of bubble plastic. Both of

Fig 13   A greenhouse lined with bubble plastic and a homemade propagating bench.

these systems are useful because they give separate areas at different temperatures which can be used for purposes other than those of rearing bedding plants.

There is one further option for the gardener with no experience of growing from seed and that is to buy pre-sown packs. These comprise a plastic tub containing compost in which the seed has already been sown. All that is required is half a dozen holes made in the base of the container, a gentle watering and then the appropriate temperature regime. It is slightly more expensive per plant than a packet of seed but is an excellent introduction for the beginner and its only real drawback is the limited range of seed which is sold in this way.

SOWING OUTSIDE

The traditional method of raising spring bedding plants such as wallflowers, is to sow the seed in prepared beds outside during the early summer

Fig 14(a)   Seed drill after germination. (b) After 'thinning out'.

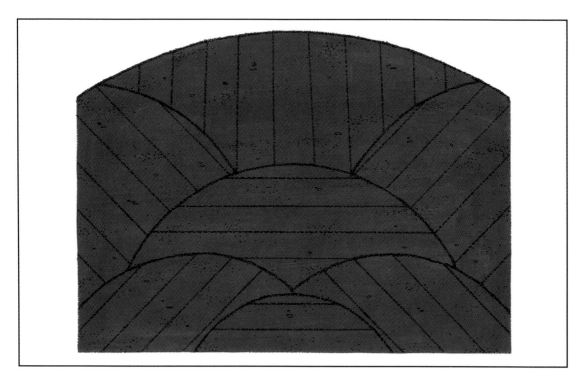

Fig 15 A bed marked out with rounded areas and seed drills at different angles to each other gives a natural look to direct-sown flowers.

and transplant the seedlings to their flowering stations during the autumn. Likewise, hardy annuals are sown where they are to flower and later thinned out to avoid overcrowding, but in this case, the sowing takes place in the spring and the plants will flower in the following summer. This system entails the removal of some seedlings at a fairly early stage whilst ensuring that the remaining plants are not damaged in the process. Although the whole operation seems appealingly simple and has the endorsement of generations of tradition, there are a number of disadvantages which leave me short of enthusiasm for sowing directly into the garden.

Identifying the weeds which will grow alongside the seedlings is difficult for amateur growers and if uncertainty causes delay, the weeds will have grown to the extent that their removal will certainly uproot some of the wanted plants. It is also true that small-seeded subjects are prone to failure, either because of disease or the fact that the seed is consumed by birds – and our feathered friends can also cause

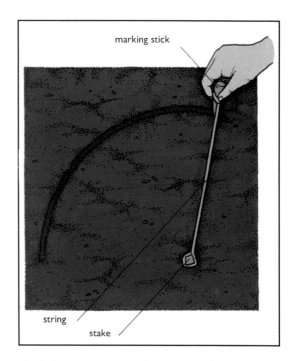

Fig 16 How to mark out circles and semi-circles in beds.

chaos when they choose to take a dust bath in the area which has been sown. Large seed may also be eaten or disturbed but it is much more likely to be successful and there are many flowers which can be grown in this way. Nonetheless, I much prefer to sow in trays, indoors or outdoors, and plant the resultant seedlings when they have reached a reasonable size. It is a fact that some annuals resent root disturbance but if the individual unit containers are used for the early stages, this problem is minimized.

If you do decide to broadcast some annual seeds, you should first thoroughly weed the bed and then lightly cultivate the top few inches, finishing off with a rake. Then, if you are aiming for a group display, mark out and designate the area for the varieties which you have chosen. If the seed is sown thinly and evenly, it will ease the later task of removing any seedlings which are too close to their companions. In the absence of timely rain, it will be necessary to water the seeds and more urgently, if a dry spell threatens whilst the seed is germinating.

SOW WHAT?

My belief is that everyone who is interested in plants will gain enormous pleasure and satisfaction from growing at least a few plants from seed but there does seem to be something which deters beginner and experienced gardener alike. Perhaps there is some aura of mystery about the techniques involved or a conviction that dis-

appointment is more common than fulfilment. Actually, neither of these ideas has any real substance but it has to be admitted that, as with all natural processes, there will be partial — and occasionally — complete failures. Usually, this is due to a lack of proper recognition of the important factors and not because success with seed is inherently difficult.

All the popular bedding plants are germinated very easily as long as the temperature and moisture requirements are met and the main problems arise with the growing-on stage where favourable cultivation must be maintained over quite a long period.

The easiest path to take if you are a beginner is to choose those subjects which grow quickly and thus can be sown and matured in late spring when conditions allow for much greater margins of error. Alyssum, marigold of all kinds and godetia are examples of bedding plants which can be sown in mid-April and will still be ready to begin flowering six weeks later. Experienced gardeners who merely want to rationalise their bedding programme can raise the quick growers — and others like ageratum, impatiens, verbenas and zinnias — and buy those plants which require a long period of growth. *Begonia semperflorens* and geraniums, for instance, need at least fourteen weeks between sowing the seed and bedding the plants out.

However much I extol the virtues and pleasures of raising plants from seed, I must acknowledge that most gardeners prefer to buy their bedding in a more advanced form.

CHAPTER 2

Buying the Plants

Although there are now some variations on the theme, four basic alternatives exist for those of you who do not wish to embark on a seed-sowing enterprise. The choice depends on your own facilities, how much trouble you can tolerate and how much your budget is for the bedding display.

SEEDLINGS

These are available from the major seed companies by mail order and increasingly at garden centres and other retail outlets. They are sometimes offered in dozens at retail establishments but the current trend in mail order is for eighty or 100 seedlings of the larger or more expensive subjects and up to 400 of the cheaper flowers such as lobelia. Often, these quantities are too large for individual gardens and a local growers' co-operative would be necessary to spread the numbers amongst friends and neighbours. Obviously, the numbers are chosen by the seed companies so that their value bears some relation to the cost of sending orders through the post and this is not necessarily a suitable arrangement for the consumer.

When the seedlings arrive through the post, they will be closely packed together and they should be pricked out into other containers as soon as possible and grown on in the usual way. The varieties which are sold in seedling form are not very numerous but the range is likely to expand and even the present situation offers a reasonable choice of the most popular flowers. Seedlings offer very good value for money and enable the gardener without germination facilities to enjoy growing the plants to maturity.

PLUGS

Known variously as 'Speedlings', 'Easyplugs' and 'Miniplugs', this is a development by specialist plant raisers in response to the increasing use of automated machinery. Plastic trays which comprise small individual 'cells' are filled, by machine, with compost and then in each of the cells a single seed is sown by a highly sophisticated sowing unit. The result is a tray of small plants, each with their own individual root system which this can easily be removed either by hand or machine.

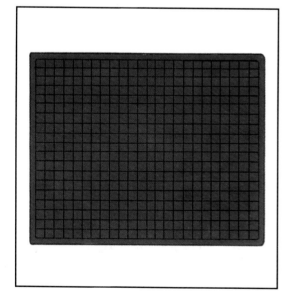

Fig 17 A plug tray with 18×24 cells.

Fig 18   A large plug, a small plug and a seedling.

The plugs are supplied by many of the seed companies through their mail order systems and are ready to plant as soon as they arrive. They are extremely simple to plant and thus the potential losses due to a conventional pricking out operation are completely removed. Plugs are very popular with the commercial bedding plant growers and it is predicted that home gardeners will buy more of them in the future, in preference to seedlings. Naturally, they are more expensive and each plantlet is about twice the price of a corresponding seedling but again the reduction of growing costs at home must be taken into consideration.

YOUNG PLANTS

Usually supplied in Jiffy 7 peat pots, these are much larger than plugs and very much more expensive. Indeed, some are offered at prices in excess of those which you might pay for mature plants and in relative terms they are often four times the price of plugs and hence eight times

Fig 19(a)   Plant in Jiffy 7.

that of seedlings. Presently, the choice is restricted to subjects for pot plants and the normally high-priced bedders such as geraniums and tuberous begonias; they are most frequently sold, by mail order, in fives or tens.

Whether buying seedlings, plugs or young plants, you are assured of the very best quality plants and this factor should be taken into account when deciding how to achieve a bedding display. All these newer forms of plants are actually grown to order for the seed companies and consequently their catalogues have closing dates, after which no orders will be taken; so early planning is necessary. It is possible that retail outlets will never offer these for sale, especially the plugs, because they have quite a short shelf-life. The quite small amount of compost in which the plants are growing means that the nutrients are quickly exhausted and the plants will suffer if they are not moved on.

Finally, it must be emphasized that however good the quality of these small plants is, they have further growth to make and their condition will deteriorate if their cultivation requirements are not met.

READY-TO-PLANT BEDDING

This category is vastly more popular than the others but, undoubtedly, the quality is much more variable and so too are the containers in which you will find bedding plants. The old wooden kipper boxes have not yet disappeared but the favourite seems to be the polystyrene 'strip' which is often linked in a block of four or five. All too often, there are far too many plants in these strips (depending on the grower) resulting in straggly and flimsy growth.

More encouraging, but more expensive, are the plants which are offered in packs of six or twelve thin plastic pots which are joined together. This is the state of the art in bedding supply because the plants have been grown individually and you can remove them from the containers without fuss or root disturbance. The use of these unit containers does not increase the growers' costs by more than a few per cent and it is my hope that the bedding plant industry will adopt this system whole-heartedly. The thin plastic unit containers do not suit the production methods of the largest growers but there are polystyrene alternatives which enable bulk handling and most importantly *allow the plants to be grown individually*.

Having released a major bee in my bonnet, it's worth considering how to judge the quality of bedding plants, even with no previous experience. Firstly, they should be uniform in leaf colour and habit of growth and those which are not compact and bushy with healthy green foliage should be ignored. They should not show any signs of pests or disease, neither should they be wilting nor be physically damaged and, in my opinion, they should not be in flower! This is, I know, one thing which is largely unheeded by the buying public and causes howls of laughter in the retail sector because it is universally recognised that plants in flower are much more easily sold than those 'in the green'. I concede that it is a difficult point to make because some subjects, like alyssum, will flower whilst they are very tiny and this is not at all detrimental to future performance. However, flowering at an early stage can be an indication of badly grown plants which have been deprived of the space and nutrients which are necessary for proper development. Of course, individual plants in the larger containers are a different proposition and for those who want it, they represent a ready-made display.

This understandable attraction of buying bedding plants in bloom does have other potential disadvantages; it encourages plant breeders to concentrate their talents on producing varieties which flower early and this does not necessarily mean that the plants' garden performance is good. Certainly there has been criticism in the industry of many varieties whose 'pack performance' is excellent but whose garden results are not.

The other unfortunate consequence of early flowers is that it entices the public to buy plants prematurely and leads to the delusion that the

Fig 19(b)   *This is what mature plants may look like, once planted out. Here, some mixed geraniums.*

season is well advanced and that planting can take place immediately. Much disappointment has resulted from premature planting and subsequent damage by the weather but the situation seems incapable of improvement. When the public wants to buy, the retailer must supply – or else lose business.

One major disadvantage of buying mature bedding plants is that they may not be properly labelled. A box of plants marked 'petunia', for instance, is not very helpful. Are they mixed colours? How tall are they? What strain of petunias are they? In the past, this situation has been bad but seems to be improving and we have to thank the British Bedding Plant Association (BBPA) for their pressure and the market leaders in the industry for setting the right example. We can only hope that all growers realise that gardeners are interested in plants and are eager for as much information as possible.

Sadly, it must be said that even if the plants are well labelled, you may not be able to find the particular variety which you want. Perhaps a very helpful shop or garden centre will make enquiries for you but otherwise you will have to go to the trouble of contacting one of the major growers and ask who is on their supply list for that particular variety.

As with all consumer matters, the power eventually lies with the buyer and you must make it known exactly what you want. If the product falls short of your expectations then complain. If the plants which you have bought fail, complain and ask for replacements or reimbursement. It may be that the failure is your fault but if you are in doubt, make sure that the supplier convinces you that it is not *his* fault. Gardeners, both amateur and professional, have a certain kinship and it is likely that you will be helped rather than ignored.

CHAPTER 3

Hardening Off

It may seem rather eccentric to devote a whole chapter to this subject but it is some measure of the importance which I give to the process of enabling plants to get a good start in their garden career.

All the half-hardy subjects and even those designated hardy which have spent the whole of their infancy in greenhouses have been protected from low temperatures and the chill factor of wind and they need to be gradually accustomed to the rigours of outdoor life. Plants are adaptable within a certain range of conditions but the change can be damaging if it is abrupt. In an ideal world, about two weeks should be devoted to

the process and each transitional stage needs a little planning.

Where the window-sill has been the location for growing plants, the next logical step is to use an unheated room in the house – remembering that maximum light is a vital factor. A garden frame is the perfect place for the following stage but where this is not available, the plants should be positioned against a south-facing house wall. There is usually little danger from daytime frosts in the run-up period before planting out but if night frosts threaten, the plants must be taken indoors until the next day.

In the greenhouse, daytime ventilation can

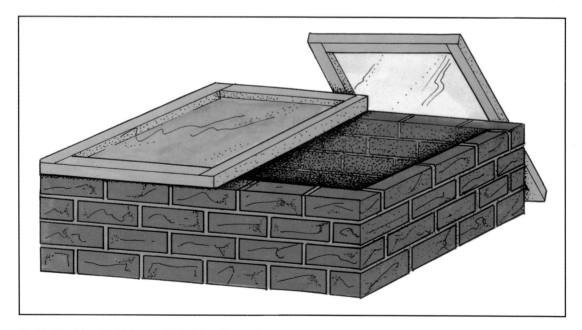

Fig 20   Traditional cold frame with brick walls and detachable lights.

Fig 21 Modern aluminium-framed cold frame on a brick base. This is ideal for hardening off tender subjects or sowing hardy plants.

Fig 22 Simple cloche made with glass and a special clip – used for hardening off.

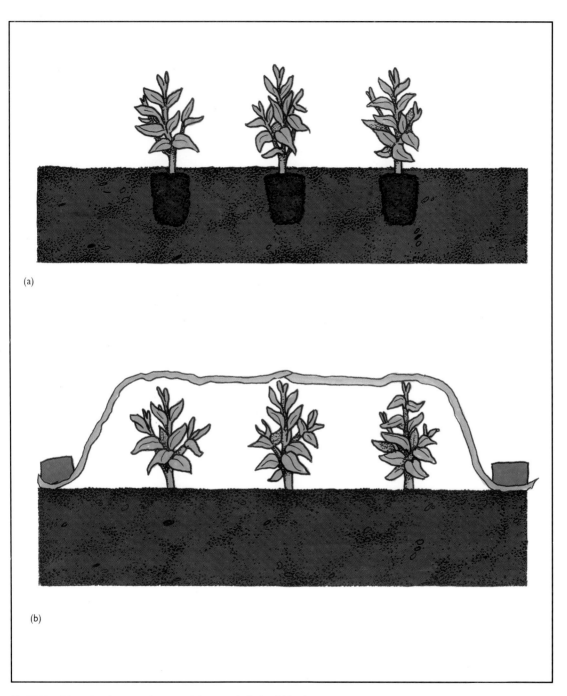

Fig 23(a)   After planting out, the top of the root ball should be just
below soil level.
        (b)   If frost threatens after planting out, drape newspaper or a light
plastic sheet on top of the plants.

23

Fig 23(c)   Once purchased plants have been hardened off, they can be placed outside in their containers, in an open position.

gradually be increased and after a few days, one of the top ventilators can be left slightly open during the night. Again, a garden frame would prove invaluable, but relatively few gardeners seem to give any priority to this piece of equipment. It does not have to be expensive and a simple home-made structure would be satisfactory.

Where mature plants have been purchased, even when they were seen to be outdoors, it should not be assumed that they have been properly hardened off and they should be put through at least an abridged version of the process when you get them home. Sometimes, purchased plants have suffered from chilling and this is not usually apparent until some time after.

The final stage in this ritual of acclimatization is reached by placing the plants, still in their containers, in an open position in the garden and this should be done when the signs are right. Inconveniently, the weather does not conform with the calendar nor with statistical predictions and you must be ready to improvise the protection strategy.

Local weather forecasts are usually accurate over the short term but there is no substitute for your own awareness and intuition. A useful ally in times of crisis is the newspaper, not for information but for placing over your bedding plants if a frost is likely; it really is effective against a light ground frost.

CHAPTER 4

Preparation, Planting and Maintenance

There is a widespread belief that whereas other plants like fruit trees, shrubs and border perennials require careful attention to preparation and planting, somehow bedding is just put into place and 'hey presto'. The myth is further compounded by the widespread piece of advice which says that good soil will lead to inferior flowering performance. Undoubtedly, the undue application of nitrogenous fertilizers will produce an excess of foliage but it will not usually reduce the number of flowers. Instead, it will increase the leaf/flower ratio and with some plants, the abundant foliage may obscure the blooms. Broadly speaking, the better the soil, the better the display, but a good soil is not one which is packed with plant food but rather one which has a good structure. This is achieved by incorporating manure and composted vegetation on a long term basis and the most important characteristic of a good soil is its ability to retain moisture.

There are some plant species which are specially adapted for existence in dry soil but most of those which we admire for their bedding qualities react badly to such conditions. They fear the worst and accelerate their flower production; they live their lives faster and die more quickly. Ideally, the soil should be permanently moist and contain adequate supplies of a wide range of nutrients which are most conveniently provided in a balanced fertilizer such as Growmore or one of the organic feeds like fish or bone meal. Liquid feed is entirely suitable but will need more frequent applications and there is

more work involved than with powder or pellet fertilizers.

PREPARATION

Preparation in most gardens entails the removal of whatever went before and a general tidying up and this certainly means the extraction of as many weeds as possible. If you want to engage in a programme of gradual soil improvement, a ½in (1cm) layer of peat can be spread over all cultivated areas. There is no need to dig it in because subsequent work and natural processes will do this for you. A dressing of about 2oz per sq yd (60g per sq m) of Growmore or similar fertilizer will be sufficient but make a mental note that for summer bedding, this application should be repeated at the beginning of August.

PLANTING

When the big day arrives, all that is needed is a watering-can, the trusty trowel and, of course, the plants. These should be generously watered in their containers at least a couple of hours before planting so that they are well charged with moisture and ready to start life in their final positions.

If your plants have been grown in individual containers, the whole business of planting will be quick, simple and pleasurable but if you have a selection of plastic strips or boxes, the compli-

Fig 24 Do not try to pull apart those plants which have grown together in a box or tray. Use a breadknife to ensure that each plant has roughly equal amounts of root.

cations will become apparent. Parkinson's Law determines that in any dozen plants which you may patiently separate, two will end up with rootballs the size of your fist and the other ten will have hardly any at all.

Patience is not the answer and you will find that ruthless expediency is a far more helpful method. Carefully lift all the plants *en masse* from the container and use a reasonably sharp breadknife to cut through the roots in fairly equal proportions. It does sound rather brutal but it is much more sympathetic than the tearing-apart technique.

Apart from the complications of bedding design, which is the subject of the next chapter, the only real problem with planting is deciding how far apart the plants should be set. I would

suggest that if, at the peak of the display, the plants are just touching each other with not a square inch of soil to be seen, then you have got it right.

I know that many gardens exemplify the 'soldiers on parade' arrangement where each plant is at arm's length from the next and if that is what you prefer, then so be it. It is your parade ground! For me, overall cover makes for a truly professional show and has the added benefit of ensuring a very limited amount of space for weeds to grow. These inevitable interlopers are easily detected, compelled to root quite shallowly and are therefore very easily pulled out.

However, the initial spacing of bedding plants is difficult to determine because different species

Fig 25   Use a ruler or measuring strip for spacing plants.

MAINTENANCE

In the realms of floral artistry, as in many other spheres of human activity, the very mention of the word maintenance leads to bored expressions and a total lack of interest. It does not have the glamour of 'design' or 'construction' but, like many gardeners, I have evolved from one who loved planning and installation and abhorred maintenance to one who has come to realize that continued attention is the principal ingredient in the art of growing plants. Cultivation is a never-ending activity rather like painting the Forth Bridge: one coat is not enough. Not that the up-keep of a bedding display entails chore after chore; observation and inspection are the two essentials and the occasional bout of admiration is only a small indulgence.

As I mentioned earlier, the most important single requirement is water because when plants are compelled to endure lengthy dry spells, it changes their metabolism. The stems harden, new growth is less readily made and this denies the plant its ability to remain juvenile and productive. If, as in 1989 and 1976 (if you can recall that summer), there are extended periods of drought, coupled with water restrictions, you will need to take emergency steps. Washing-up water and second-hand bath water are perfectly harmless to plants in the short term and although it may be an irksome task, it is surely preferable to watching the premature demise of a promising floral pageant. Of course, if there are no restrictions on the use of hose-pipes then just make the connection and turn on the tap, always remembering that if a sprinkler is being used, it takes a long time to simulate a shower of rain. The only hard and fast rule is drench, do not dribble.

Pinching

Soon after planting your bedding scheme, it is advisable to have a close look at all the plants to see whether or not the new growth is as it should be. Most modern strains of the dwarf subjects have

will achieve differing dimensions and better soil builds bigger plants. An additional aspect to the dilemma is the fact that separate strains of the same flower often have varying levels of vigour and, just to make things quite hopeless, some colours within the same strain can be different sizes.

The perfect spacing of bedding plants is like all other kinds of perfection – unattainable. Nevertheless, it is something which you can aspire to, using a ruler or measuring strip (*see* Fig 25), and the experience gathered from successive seasons is the best guide-line. In the meantime, I think you should err on the close side because slight overcrowding does give a distinctly natural look and, as we all learned at school, nature hates vacuums.

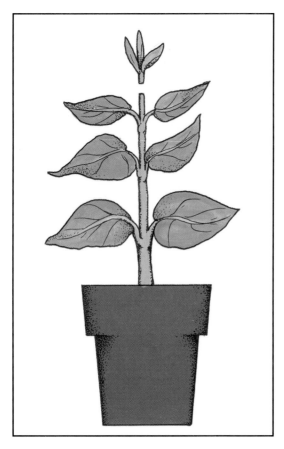

Fig 26(a) Pinching out the growing tip to encourage bushy growth.

been bred for compact and bushy growth but sometimes, especially if the cultivation has been inferior, the plants may be 'leggy' with elongated and spindly growth. If this is so, the top inch or so of the growing tip should be removed and this will induce a bushier habit.

Some gardeners like to do this initially with antirrhinums, marigolds and nicotianas but it does mean that the first flowers will be delayed. Plants so treated will very often be much more even in their subsequent flowering. It is certainly wise to use this technique throughout the season where the shoots of any plants have become too long and out of balance with their companions.

Dead-Heading

This is a vital piece of maintenance which is often neglected and widely misunderstood. It is not the action of a supremely tidy gardener who cannot bear to see dead flowers blighting the display and wishes to keep everything in pristine condition; dead-heading does help to maintain the freshness of the beds but there is another, more fundamental, principle involved. Plants which flower – and they are the vast majority – have only one purpose to their existence and that is to perpetuate the species. Flowers attract insects to pollinate their seed heads which then develop viable seed for the next generation and, put rather simply, if the plant is allowed to produce large amounts of seed, its purpose in life is complete and therefore its level of productive activity will diminish. So, if you remove the seed heads quite regularly, the plant will continue to produce new seed and new flowers as well.

There are some helpful exceptions to the dead-heading rule such as *begonia semperflorens* and impatiens; both of these are 'self-cleaning' which means that the seed heads drop off before they ripen and, consequently, these subjects flower continuously without the need for dead-heading. Some of the modern marigolds, the triploids, are sterile and do not produce seed, but I would certainly advise you to remove the dead flowers – they look unsightly and tend to go mouldy during wet weather, which can affect the rest of the plant.

A two-pronged campaign of ensuring adequate moisture for the plants *and* regular dead-heading will definitely extend the summer show by a matter of weeks and more than compensates for the amount of work involved. However, not all flowers can be conveniently dead-headed and with others, it is completely impractical. With the tiny flowers of alyssum and lobelia, it would be like picking Christmas tree needles off the carpet whereas with antirrhinums, it is essential to remove the whole spike as soon as the top flower has faded, otherwise there will be no later flushes of bloom. As with

Fig 26(b)   If you follow the instructions set out in this chapter, your garden will be ready to accept new recruits!

every job, a little practice will improve efficiency and even the stubborn heads, like those of petunias, can be detached quickly and without damage to the plant. Marigolds are easily dealt with but geraniums need different treatment; the whole cluster should be removed together with the stalk, which can be broken off with downward pressure at its junction with the main stem.

I shall not try and convince you that dead-heading is good for the soul but it can have a certain therapeutic value and there is the consolation that it will increase your return on the bedding investment.

Weeding

Whole books have been devoted to these garden squatters but I believe that anything more than a few lines would give undue prominence to what is more of an irritation than a curse. The sight of a neglected garden can be daunting but one which has received a modicum of regular cultivation is easily kept within the bounds of decency. Not that you can keep it weed-free, because even if they are not to be seen, they are certainly there, lurking and waiting for a lack of vigilance. I am a firm supporter of the 'pull'em out system' and I think the hoe should be treated like a parasol and only be brought out in dry, sunny weather. If it is used in wet soil, the hoe becomes the perfect implement for moving weeds from one place to another. When conditions are dry, it exposes weed roots to desiccation or decapitates the offender but in careless hands and crowded beds, it is lethal to friend and foe alike. Of course, hand weeding really is good for the soul . . .

CHAPTER 5

Bedding Design

It is with some trepidation that I embark on this chapter because I strongly believe that your home is your castle and what you do in the castle grounds is entirely up to you. Anyway, all gardens have a different permanent framework of plants and obviously require varying treatment. I always keep one bed which is planted solely with summer bedding but you may have neither the space nor the inclination to do the same. In the sophisticated world of design, there are acknowledged rules which govern form and colour but I am not convinced that they are relevant to domestic gardens. Most important – and to use the contemporary phrase – is to 'do your own thing'; you are not marketing a product and you are not trying to please your neighbours – though compliments are nice – so please yourself.

It seems to me that most garden displays concentrate on a mixture of colours without bothering much about matching and this is almost certainly because most gardeners buy seed mixtures. Many of these do not work well and even the formula mixes that have been devised by the seed companies leave a distinct memory of patchiness. In the warehouse of the seed company, the mixture in a hundredweight bag may have the colours in beautifully balanced proportions but by the time it is distributed amongst thousands of half-gram packets, the situation may have changed. Further imbalance can occur if you only use two dozen plants from the packet or buy a dozen mixed plants from the garden centre.

The worst situation can arise with mixtures which might contain ten or a dozen colours but you will find that *Begonia semperflorens*, for instance, has a restricted range of reds, pinks and white which almost always look right. On the other hand you may be unlucky if you buy a dozen begonias and find that there are seven pinks, four reds and one white. To many people,

Fig 27   Unless you are prepared to lift spring bulbs and plants after flowering, it is more expedient to plant them all in small groups rather than en masse.

Fig 28   Not everyone will agree that these two colours combine well but the French marigold 'Aurora Fire' and ageratum 'Blue Champion' are bedding companions.

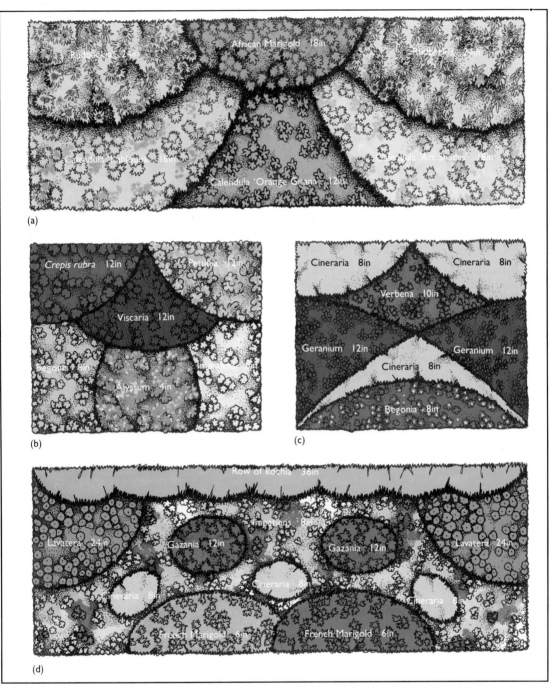

Fig 29 It is a good idea to draw plans of your flower beds so that you can experiment with designs. Try different colour combinations and various groups of plants which differ in height and form. If you keep each year's plan, you can note how successful your designs have been. A few ideas for designs and plants are given – the measurements refer to plant height: (a) orange and gold shades; (b) pinks; (c) red and silver; (d) multi-coloured groups.

31

this may be of no real consequence but I do think that it puts the display in the hands of providence and not in your own.

My own preference, for beds which are solely devoted to summer bedding, is for one of three basic schemes:

(i)   A single colour
(ii) A single colour but with a variety of shades
(iii) Either of the above but with one additional and compatible colour

These suggestions are based purely on colour and with (ii), for example, pink antirrhinums could associate with pink petunias and would give the extra dimension of two differing forms in flower and foliage. I think you will also find that if pink, especially light pink, is used as the basis for a colour scheme, it is hard to make a mistake. Pink combines well with most of the spectrum and is very compatible with red which is, I suspect, the favourite garden colour.

Red geraniums or salvias, with blue lobelia and white alyssum is a combination which has out-lived all its critics; I also think that it makes a strik-ing flag but a strident bedding scheme. I am not suggesting that red and blue should not be used together but I venture to say that one of them should dominate and perhaps a 'mediator' should be added to soften the sensory assault. The ideal mediator, for this and indeed any strong contrasts, is the silver foliage of *Cineraria maritima* and most superb bedding displays that I have seen contain this plant. One of the most memorable patterns was in a garden which con-tained a pastel-pink impatiens and cineraria 'Silver Dust' in roughly equal proportions, as well as a scarlet geranium used as a dot plant.

Vivid colours make the most eye-catching spectacles but the impact does diminish when you become accustomed to it and later even boredom can result. It is a contentious and emotive topic but the secret of successful design does seem to be the simple use of a background with areas of highlights. Conversely, it can look very appealing, though more daring, with the

Fig 30   Wherever you see professional bedding, Cineraria maritima *is bound to be present; here seen as an edging at Springfields.*

Fig 31   In the town centre at Bakewell in Derbyshire, kochia are used as dot plants, interplanted with petunias.

main coverage in a strong colour and the focal points in more subdued hues.

Colour, like everything else in the garden, needs blending in and there is no substitute for a touch of natural flair. If, like me, you lack this attribute, then you must experiment and learn from experience – your own and that of others. Looking at other gardens, public and private, will add to your knowledge and although you may not be able to duplicate those that you admire, they will give you the opportunity to compare different plant and colour associations. The reassuring feature of bedding schemes is that they form a tapestry which is easily unpicked to reveal a clean canvas, ready for a fresh start.

Most of the above comments have been directed towards the use of areas which are devoted to bedding plants but modern domestic gardens rely on mixed and more informal arrangements. They almost always contain a few conifers, flowering shrubs, some border perennials and, of course, the statutory rose-bed. All the plants in the garden have their peak of interest and periods when they are at best dull and at worst an eyesore. This is when bedding subjects can sparkle in centre stage whilst the new focus of attention allows other plants to rest in the wings.

Rose-beds are very suitable for cosmetic treatment because, while they provide really beautiful flowers, few people would claim that the bushes are at all attractive. At their best, they comprise gaunt stems partially clothed in unremarkable foliage and at worst, they resemble a collection of vicious weapons protruding from the soil. What is needed is the camouflage of spring flowers like wallflowers or forget-me-nots to hide the newly pruned skeletons and, later, a carpet of summer plants to obscure the naked lower stems. There is often a bare expanse of ground between the bushes and bearing in mind that the rose bloom is produced 2–3ft (61–91cm) above the soil, there are dozens of summer bedders which will cheerfully transform the conventional rose-bed. Most rose-beds contain a number of different varieties with various colours and an

Fig 32 A small suburban garden is given another dimension by using taller dot plants; in this case, standard fuchsias.

Fig 33 Another view of the same garden shows how varied the effect can be.

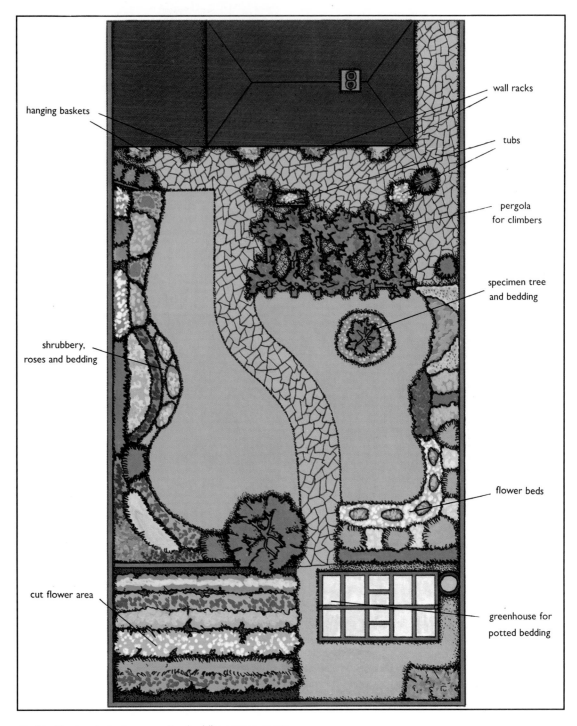

hanging baskets

wall racks

tubs

pergola
for climbers

specimen tree
and bedding

shrubbery,
roses and bedding

flower beds

cut flower area

greenhouse for
potted bedding

Fig 34   Garden design incorporating bedding arrangements.

Fig 35 The professional touch in a garden scheme is evident in the close planting. The main components here are tagetes, 'Non Stop' begonias and 'Solar' African marigolds.

Fig 36 An exotic look is supplied by the contrasting form and colour of canna amongst the uniformity of pink geraniums.

underlying canopy of subdued hues will help to· unify the whole scene.

The usual approach where perennial subjects are situated is to choose bedding plants which are sympathetic to the colour and the height of the permanent residents. This obviously means that there must be some space between the herbaceous plantings and if you enjoy the results of temporary additions, you may have to reduce the size of the perennial clumps in subsequent years. It is impossible to generalize about how to use bedding in these situations; sometimes single plants will suffice but, usually, small groups will be preferable. Some flowering shrubs, just like roses, are subject to annual pruning and can be rather

ugly at certain times of the year and here again, some thoughtful use of annuals will divert attention away from the results of secateur surgery. Other shrubs, however, like choisya and elaeagnus, are permanently good-looking and they serve as an excellent backdrop for colourful bedders.

Walls and fences present opportunities which should not be wasted because they allow the display to be elevated and increase the variety of plants which can be featured. Many house walls boast a clematis but this lovely subject is not always in flower and there are quite a number of annual climbers which will happily use the clematis as a temporary support. Pyracantha is

35

*Fig 36(b) Variations in height and colour will give more depth to a
border, as demonstrated here by a combination of asters, antirrhinums
and allysum.*

often planted against a wall and its open habit of
growth makes it very suitable for a climbing com-
panion which can be removed before the
autumn, when the bright berries grab the
limelight.

There are infinite facets to garden design but
there is no need to be daunted by this prospect.
Make sure that you give some attention to variety of form, particularly with foliage, and ensure
that there is some variation in the height of those
subjects which are used in beds; then you can
concentrate on colour. There has been an increasing trend towards separate colour planning

and more horticultural outlets are becoming
aware of it. Seed companies too, are joining the
movement by offering more packets of the
individual colours in a wide range of varieties. Of
course, this in itself is not completely helpful
because customers who want two or three
colours have to pay two or three times the cost
of a mixed packet. One company, however, has
pioneered in this respect by offering one packet
which contains a number of colours which have
been separately wrapped. I hope that the idea
succeeds and is adopted by the other seed companies.

CHAPTER 6

Tubs, Troughs, Baskets and Boxes

Gardening in containers has become increasingly popular in recent times and this is not surprising; it can add to the garden display or provide interest and spectacle for those who have no gardens. Backyards, paths and driveways are all barren areas but a well-placed and imaginatively planted receptacle can transform the appearance of home, factory or office. There is a considerable variety of containers and the only limiting factors are the initial cost or the talent necessary for improvisation.

TUBS AND TROUGHS

Undoubtedly, stone is the most desirable material but this type of container has become highly collectable and the prices are usually prohibitive. Even those made from reconstituted stone are very expensive but they will last a lifetime or two. The weight is also a problem but I have noticed that platforms on castors are now sold and I find the notion of plants on wheels rather appealing.

Concrete is the most common material for 'reproduction' tubs, which are also very heavy, and the initial newness is starkly disagreeable. A few weeks in the elements will tone them down but if you wish to accelerate the ageing process, water the exterior with a liquid manure and sprinkle some fine soil over the nooks and crannies. This will enable mosses to gain a foothold and help to give a tasteful, weathered look.

Terracotta has made a strong come back and there are some beautiful designs both traditional and modern. Of course, they are likely to crack with careless handling and there is a danger of damage caused by severe frosts but this is not so true of those manufactured by modern methods.

Wood is a superb choice for garden containers and has the advantage of being quite light and although it will rot if neglected, an annual treatment with preservative will defer decay almost indefinitely.

The ubiquitous plastic urn, trough, sink or tub is scorned by many but it has to be conceded that some of the better quality items are convincing and remarkably robust. The main deficiency, particularly of those which have a plinth, is that they are so light as to be unstable. Prejudice apart, it is inescapably true that plastic is a most versatile and practical material for garden use.

Soil-based compost is the best for this kind of container, not only because the extra weight will improve the stability of plastic items but also because plant nutrients are retained for much longer. This important attribute makes it the best medium for all containers with the exception of hanging baskets but the extra cost factor is a deterrent. Use the more common peat composts by all means but remember that feeding will be necessary much earlier. If you have a number of containers and want to economize on composts, make your own with moss peat, vermiculite and a pack of chemicals which you can buy from most horticultural retailers. And what about garden soil? If it is good enough for garden

Plastic – versatile, but liable to crack.

Concrete – heavy, but long-lasting.

Reconstituted stone – most elegant, but expensive.

Fibreglass – similar to plastic, but more durable.

Terracotta – associates well with plants, but liable to crack and chip.

Wood – ideal, but remember to treat it annually with a preservative.

Fig 37   A selection of the different types of containers available for the garden.

plants, why not for those same plants in containers? Well, I have used it myself, mixed with a generous quantity of peat and supplemented with a balanced fertilizer and I can think of no reason why you should not try it. Traditionalists will not concur but there's no harm in some occasional gardening heresy. Do ensure, however, that the final mix does drain well and keep a regular eye on the plants, giving more feed when it seems necessary.

Plants for Tubs

Like everything else in the garden, personal preferences will determine what plants are used

Fig 39   Petunia 'Pink Cascade' looks superb when planted in edging beds, window boxes, hanging baskets and tubs.

Fig 38   Variegated plectranthus makes a most versatile foliage 'filler' which is equally at home in a pot, hanging basket, tub or in flowering beds.

but I would say that many displays in containers lack 'body'. Usually, this is because the selection of material does not include some foliage subjects which add weight and provide a balance to the flower power. Plectranthus, especially the variegated type, and the various varieties of helichrysum are ideal for this purpose and the silver leaves of *Cerastium tomentosum* make a lovely foil for strong or delicate colours.

Suitable flowering plants are legion but it is sensible to choose from those with a long period of bloom and also to plan for some variation in terms of height and habit. Tuberous begonias, petunias, geraniums and impatiens are always in flower and are certain to please, but there are dozens of other bedding plants which will serve well. Tall plants are generally less fitting but it depends very much on the size of the tub. Troughs and smaller containers look superb with single variety plantings of one colour and the impatiens would be difficult to improve on, even if the situation were partially shaded.

WINDOW BOXES

These have largely fallen from favour perhaps because most modern windows open out and the old sash windows are fast disappearing, but

39

Fig 40 Window box in spring with colour provided by pansies and Alyssum saxatile.

the installation of window boxes is also a problem. They need very strong brackets fixed to the wall and these are quite expensive. However, once installed and suitably planted, window boxes will really enhance the looks of a house. Plastic boxes are available but they may not be of suitable dimensions, in which case, wooden boxes which have been treated with preservative are more satisfactory. One important point is to make sure that the drainage holes are towards the front of the boxes, otherwise the water which passes through will run down the house wall.

All low-growing and trailing plants are suitable for window boxes but unless foliage subjects are favoured, selection is better made from bedding plants which flower continuously. You may also want to consider flowers which will complement the colour of the exterior paint-work.

HANGING BASKETS

Wire baskets used to be the only hanging containers that gardeners could use but nowadays the most commonly used baskets are made from plastic. This probably reflects the difficulty and expense of obtaining good-quality moss and also the fact that lining and filling the wire baskets is a painstaking job which requires some patient application. The plastic products come in all sizes and designs, and include some which have planting holes around the main body of the basket. Of course, a well-planted basket will have flowers

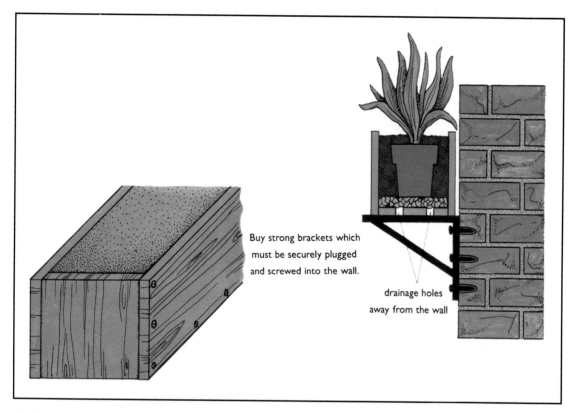

Buy strong brackets which
must be securely plugged
and screwed into the wall.

drainage holes
away from the wall

*Fig 41 It may be difficult to buy window boxes which are the right size.
You can make your own with thick timber – at least ¾in (2cm) thick –
and fix it to a wall with screws. Use a wood preservative to finish it off.*

and foliage cascading from the top with the intention of concealing the actual container. Wire baskets do lose moisture very quickly and, on this account, I have seen many which have an inner lining of plastic sheet instead of moss. At first, this is not attractive but successful growth will soon obscure the aesthetic deficiencies. It is also possible to buy fibre liners, which are usually brown, and these are entirely satisfactory for wire baskets.

Apart from those which are ridiculously shallow, plastic baskets are very practical and many of them are of pleasing design and colour. Some have an attached 'saucer' which acts as a most useful water reservoir and, if carefully used, can prevent drips.

The best composts to use for all kinds of hang-

ing baskets are peat-based because this material is lighter in weight and retains moisture better than the loam composts. The latest innovation is composts which have been specifically prepared for hanging baskets and contain fertilizers which are released slowly and over a long period of time. However, it would be unwise to expect these composts to provide an adequate supply of nutrients over the whole life of a basket display and additional feeding will be necessary.

Plants for Hanging Baskets

Everyone's priority is for trailing plants and this is as it should be but it is a mistake not to give some consideration to upright subjects, especially for the centre of the basket. Trailing lobelia seems to be the favourite choice and it does make a splendid show but remember that it is drought-prone and regular dryness will hasten its demise. The answer is to ensure that lobelia is not the main component of the display – and when it does fade away, it can be cut out without affecting the overall effect and the other plants will expand to take its place.

Impatiens, fuchsia and pendulous begonias are perfect basket plants but fuchsias love moist conditions and they will give very obvious signs if they are under stress. Zonal geraniums are excellent for a centre-piece and the ivy-leaf kinds really come into their own as basket subjects; in addition, both of these are very tolerant of dryness.

Single variety plantings in one colour will always attract admiration but most people favour a mixture of plants and colours. Here too, foliage balance is desirable. As well as *helichrysum* and *plectranthus*, you will find that *Sedum linare*, *lysimachia* and *Glechoma hederacea variegata* make superb trailing specimens. The latter is sometimes listed as *Nepeta hederacea* and is unusual in that it trails absolutely vertically. Whilst on the subject of foliage, I must mention that the baskets which have attracted most attention in my garden have been the ones without any flowers at all.

One final point about hanging baskets. If a prominent plant fails badly or fades prematurely, don't feel apprehensive about replacing it. It will require cutting a hole in the compost, preferably with a sharp knife and after replacing the compost, a new plant can be inserted.

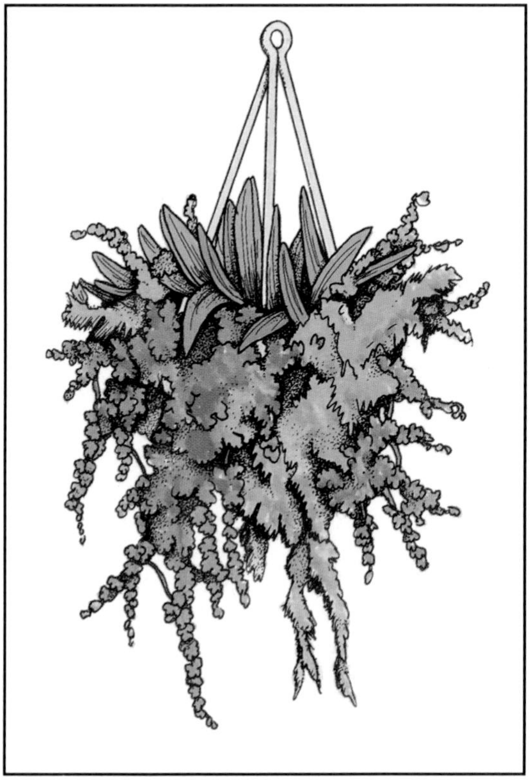

Fig 42 A hanging basket containing green foliage can make a very attractive display.

WATERING CONTAINERS

The major problem associated with all kinds of container gardening is watering and it can be especially irksome with hanging baskets. Even in a season which has reasonable rainfall, containers will always need attention, partly because overhanging foliage will prevent water from reaching the compost and also because they are densely planted. It is possible to arrange a drip-feed to tubs from a hose-pipe but the advantage is probably outweighed by the trouble involved. A disciplined approach to watering seems to be the inevitable price which we have to pay for the joy of containerised displays.

A full-sized watering-can is useless for hanging baskets and even a small one is unhelpful for those which are fairly high. Here, I am sure that a flexible plastic bottle is the most simple and versatile device.

A final thought about containers in general is the possibility of using them throughout the year. Summer use is obvious but it seems a pity not to have a spring show as well. The larger bulbs of tulips and daffodils are ideal for large tubs and can be accompanied by winter-flowering pansies,

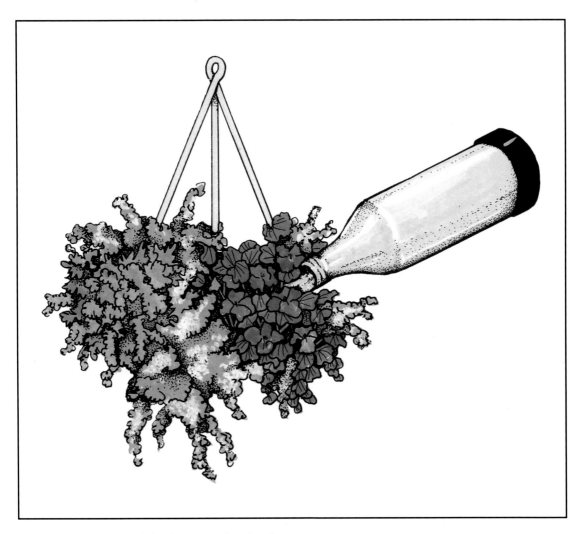

Fig 43   Use a flexible plastic bottle to water hanging plants.

dwarf wallflowers and perhaps Brompton stocks. There is a smaller range of subjects for hanging baskets but pansies and aubretia are sure to please and a couple of the hardy ivies will add some variation.

The essential thing is to try your garden favourites in containers and use a little imagina- tion to achieve colourful combinations and in- dividual highlights. Very few bedding plants will fail in containers and an adventurous approach can bring some exciting results. Successful plant associations on the small scale will encourage you to experiment in the larger format of the garden itself.

43

CHAPTER 7

Parasites – Insects and Others

All diseases are parasitic by nature because they live on other organisms and many garden insects fall into this category for the same reason but I do believe that there is an unfortunate pre-occupation with these potential problems.

DISEASES

There are some dreadful ailments which can afflict plants but they are uncommon in the domestic garden and I do not propose to mention anything which is unlikely to be encountered. If some unidentifiable disease becomes apparent, the best thing to do is seek expert advice either from the local authority horticultural adviser or from experienced gardeners in your locality. The latter can be found in specialist plant societies or allotment groups and it is also possible to get advice from a nearby garden centre.

The everyday complaints – which are almost inevitable at some time in a plant's life – are invariably caused by a variety of different fungal diseases. It becomes noticeable that some plants are more susceptible than others and the cause can often be traced to weather conditions. The first ailment to be mentioned, however, is usually the fault of the gardener and can normally be prevented.

Damping Off

This, ocurs when young seedlings are exposed to high humidity and crowded conditions but it can be prevented by careful preparation for the seed-sowing operation. Using Cheshunt compound as an initial and subsequent drench will often deter

the fungus but it is vital to disinfect all receptacles and use a sterilized compost. Damping off is usually detected when seedlings appear to wilt. Careful examination will show that the damage occurs just above soil level and if the infection is advanced, the seedling will collapse and wither.

Botrytis

Wet seasons make this trouble almost inevitable but it need not cause great concern. It usually attacks the large double flowers of plants such as marigolds and dahlias and the wooly mould may spread to the stems and leaves if the flower is not removed. If the condition is widespread, the only effective recourse is to a fungicide such as one which contains benomyl.

Mildew

Two types make this a bewildering complaint because one is prevalent in wet conditions and the other is more common in a dry season. Downy mildew is the one which favours the wet and powdery mildew is the unwelcome visitor during dry weather but both can be controlled by fungicide sprays.

INSECTS

Whereas any disease, by definition, is bad, the same cannot be said of insect life. Bedding plants will certainly become host to the various creatures which will feed on them – that is the nature of things – but it is unlikely that severe damage will be caused. If a real infestation occurs, you can use a proprietary insecticide but there are other options and other considerations.

Greenfly

If you eradicate greenfly from your garden, you make the whole area inhospitable to those creatures which make a living from aphids. Greenfly are most unlikely to debilitate your bedding plants; anyway, they are usually decimated by a heavy shower of rain which washes them to the ground and they are largely unable to return. My first reaction to a build-up of aphids is to use a spray of soapy water; it removes them incompletely, but cleanly! You may also use one of the environmentally safe products which are based on insecticidal soap.

In a world which is being made untenable for man – by man – it disturbs me to envisage a beautiful garden which is toxic to insect life. It is rather like Snow White's apple – inviting but deadly. Of course, it is possible to use insecticides which are relatively harmless to all but the 'target' but many of the sprays which are commonly used deal death and destruction to most insect life. That includes such desirables as lacewings, hover-flies, ladybirds, butterflies, moths and perhaps most regretably, bees of all kinds.

Caterpillars

Caterpillars may deserve a slightly different treatment from that of greenfly but I would not advocate full-scale warfare. Many of them become gorgeous moths or butterflies and only a few are likely to make a meal out of your bedding plants. A few brassicas in the vegetable patch will happily occupy the pretty but much maligned cabbage white and any other caterpillars are not likely to be so plentiful. If you must take action, I recommend the following in ascending order of preference:

(i) Spray or powder insecticide
(ii) Pick them off with heavy pressure between thumb and forefinger

(iii) Pick them off, put them in a jar with some leaves and give them to the little boy next door

Earwigs

I have never heard of earwigs reaching epidemic proportions but even one of these little articulated tanks can make a mess of prize dahlia blooms. In a bedding display, I doubt whether they will ever cause noticeable damage, but if you decide to hunt them, sprinkle insecticide around their likely lairs. Otherwise, you can adopt the old-fashioned technique of packing an inverted plant pot with straw or dried grass – but how you dispose of your captives is up to you.

Capsid Bugs

In some years capsid bugs can cause cosmetic damage to the leaves of many plants but the effects are difficult to counter without a perpetual spray programme. The insect punctures the leaf tissue and you will find small holes, especially in the young foliage. The damage is never wholesale, however, and is no threat to the well-being of the plant. Froghoppers feed in the same way but again, no action is needed unless you find the 'cuckoo spit' offensive.

Leaf miner

Leaf miner can be a considerable irritant especially to chrysanthemum growers because of the grubs which tunnel between the outer membranes of the leaves. If an attack remains unchecked, the disfigurement can be thoroughly depressing but if spray action is taken at the first signs, the damage limitation is worthwhile. Systemic sprays, from which the poisons are absorbed by the leaves, are the most effective control but unfortunately, many of these insecticides are not recommended for use on chrysanthemums.

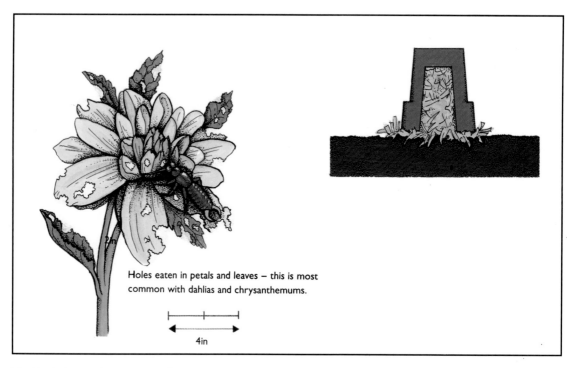

Holes eaten in petals and leaves – this is most common with dahlias and chrysanthemums.

4in

Fig 44   An inverted plant pot stuffed with straw or pieces of newspaper makes an effective trap for earwigs.

tunnels

Fig 45   Leaf miner larvae tunnel and feed between the two 'skins' of leaves. Their damage shows as creamy lines which later turn brown. Badly affected leaves should be removed.

Slugs

These are the only garden pests which need in-depth discussion because, for most gardeners, they represent the most destructive adversary of all. Utterly defenceless, slugs and to a lesser extent snails, are relentless consumers of all soft-tissue plants and although they are vulnerable to attack, the sheer number of these marauding molluscs is awe-inspiring. Some years ago, the *Gardening Which* publication told the story of one gardener with a ¼ acre plot who was determined to do a slug census. He captured 47,000 in the first year, 36,000 the next and in the third year, the catch was 61,000. In the fourth year, he gave up after a further 49,000 had been caught and I'm sorry to report that he did not receive a Nobel prize for his dedication to gardening science. Perhaps his garden embraced a national breeding ground but other research has shown that many gardens will have slug populations which exceed 100 per sq m.

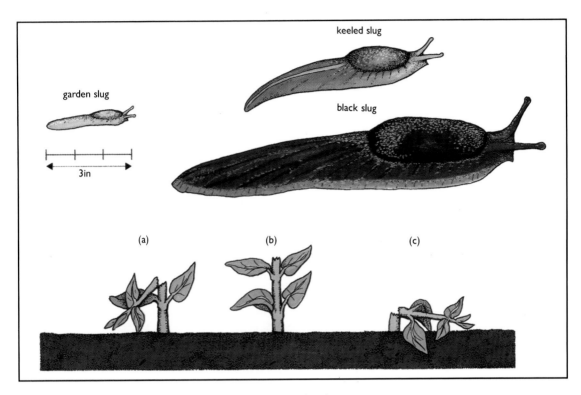

*Fig 46   Damage to plants: (a) The stem is eaten half-way up the plant –
it should survive. (b) The tip is destroyed – it should survive. (c) The stem
is severed below the lowest leaves – this plant is unlikely to survive.*

Since it is one of the slowest creatures on this planet and has no body protection, the slug is easy prey for any predators but because it is mostly nocturnal, birds are not very useful allies for the gardener. Hedgehogs may be the most effective, natural ally that gardeners have but unfortunately, they are not numerous in urban areas.

For all practical purposes there are only two kinds of slugs – small and large – and their threat to bedding and other plants is directly proportional to the size of their bodies, and hence their mouths. Their dietary preference is for the newly emerged shoots of perennial subjects, often eaten underground, or recently planted bedding. With a recorded top speed of 1lyd (10m) per hour, their progress is painstaking but the damage which they inflict can move gardeners to

tears. All soft vegetation seems at risk and they will often climb to reach fresh leaves and shoots but the threat to bedding plants is at ground level. Young bedding plants are totally edible and if slugs eat the stems at the point where they enter the soil, the plant is destroyed.

A counter-offensive based on slug pellets has come under some criticism because of the possible effects on other wildlife but research has indicated that birds and animals are unlikely to eat the pellets or the slugs which have succumbed to the poisonous bait. Metaldehyde and methiocarb are the usual poisons and the latter is more effective but much more toxic. It should be mentioned that many brands of pellets also contain substances which will deter other creatures from eating them.

A traditional remedy is to sprinkle cinders

around the plants but these are not easily obtained and slugs have been observed ignoring the discomfort. Anyway, nature has equipped them with the means of laying their own mucous highway so that they can glide over obstacles, natural and man-made. In recent years, a tape has been patented which is impregnated with an anti-slug compound and can be used to mark the no-go areas. Inconveniently, many slugs have underground capabilities and the potency of the tape is diminished by rainfall. Rain is also the bane of those liquid slug-killers which are watered over the ground.

Beer traps are also advocated but the success of this method probably owes more to mythology than reality although some slugs are certainly caught. The system is impractical because the traps would need to be placed every foot or so around the garden and ground beetles, which do predate slugs, would also fall victim to the traps. If you must use these traps, then I suggest that you try some other liquid lures and think of another way of deploying surplus beer.

I realize that I may be accused of a paranoid attitude towards slugs but I believe that there is a strong kindred spirit amongst those who tend gardens which are wet. My conclusion is that where the slug problem is severe, pellets must be at least part of the offensive, otherwise plant losses could be serious. If, for a few nights after you have set out your bedding plants, you are prepared to spend ten minutes with a torch and a pair of scissors, the results will be worthwhile. It seems rather barbaric but it is an environ-mentally safe method, much more humane than using salt which doesn't adversely affect nearby plants.

Controlling the trespass of dogs and cats in the garden is an emotive topic and rather than lose friends, two- and four-legged, I would prefer to leave you to your own devices. The many products which are sold to ward off domestic pets do not seem to have much effect and perhaps this is a chance to try some applied psychology. Man's first and second best friends are creatures of regular habits and if you demonstrate clearly, but kindly, that you resent their presence, they will often omit your garden from their normal itinerary. If they will not stay away . . . See if you can persuade them to eat slugs!

Whatever steps you take, something will go wrong in the garden but with reasonable vigilance, most troubles can be minimized. If you get into the habit of just looking, often and carefully; the accumulated experience will be invaluable. You will quickly learn to see when something is wrong – a slightly drooping stem, a few curled leaves or inferior growth. Regular observation will enable you to identify a plant which differs from its companions, perhaps because of insect attack or disease. If you find one which spoils the display or seems to have a disease which may be transmitted to the others, then pull it out – this is when you will appreciate the merit of growing some spare plants in pots. These substitutes are excellent for decoration in the greenhouse, conservatory, home or simply outside the back door, but when a replacement is needed in the garden, they become invaluable.

CHAPTER 8

The Spring Garden

This book is mostly concerned with summer bedding but most gardeners will wish to have displays which occupy as much of the year as possible and this natural desire does present difficulties. Public parks have major plantings of spring subjects which are removed *en masse* at the end of May and replaced by summer bedding. Some of the spring material is consigned to the compost heap but a great deal is transplanted in nursery beds in readiness for the next spring. Most domestic gardens do not have sufficient space to follow this routine and there is

Fig 47(a)   Tulip beds in Stamford Park, Ashton under Lyne. In parks, tulips often stand unaccompanied but in the garden they are better planted with wallflowers or other companions.

an understandable reluctance to throw away polyanthus and other high-cost perennials.

The alternative is to have a scattered framework of spring colour provided by perennial flowers and bulbs which have naturalized and which can then be supplemented by temporary subjects. If, as I have done to my cost, your borders are filled with bulbs, there is a long period after flowering when the dying foliage is far from attractive but, even worse, it becomes extremely awkward to plant the summer bedding because you cannot get a trowel between the bulbs! On the other hand, small groups of daffodils or crocuses are easily disguised by subsequent plantings and the transition from one season to the next is not blighted by brown leaves.

One drawback to spring bedding plants is that most of them will have to be treated as perennials or biennials, which means that the seed must be sown in the previous spring or summer. Enthusiasts may not complain but others may resent the additional work and the complication of cultivating more plants until autumn. Of course, mature plants can be purchased for setting out towards the end of the year but the choice of material is often disappointing. Even if you are buying seed, the options are quite limited and perhaps plant breeders in the future may direct their talents to providing more variety for spring bedding.

There is another dilemma which you will face, usually in the late spring, when the wallflowers, pansies and sweet-williams are looking magnificent and the summer bedding plants are ready for planting. It is a difficult decision to make and whereas some people leave well alone, others operate strictly according to the calendar: on 30 May, everything comes out. My inclination is to let flowering plants flower, and I can only add that whilst mass displays will exacerbate this situation, a more fragmented deployment of spring plants will avoid this pitfall. The other point to make is that well-grown summer bedding plants will not come to any harm if they are not planted for a week or so, as long as they are properly watered.

We all tend to look on spring as a very separate experience but in nature the seasons do not have strictly defined boundaries and you need to plan the year as a whole and to use the calendar as a general guide. The flowering periods of many plants overlap the seasons and can be invaluable in maintaining a continuity of display.

THE PLANTS

The plants in the following chapters are listed alphabetically under their Latin names except where the popular names are universally acknowledged. This is a source of irritation to some gardeners but I have tried to follow the system which is commonly used in plant and seed catalogues and I hope that it enables easy reference. The plant names are followed by an abbreviation which indicates how the plants are grown for bedding purposes and this may contradict the precise description of their natural characteristics. For instance, wallflowers and antirrhinums are strictly perennial by nature but after their first flowering season, the plants decline greatly and are unsuitable as permanent residents of the garden. Other subjects may fall into more than one category.

Hardy Annuals HA The hardy annuals are tenacious plants which can survive low temperatures and may be sown outdoors, generally in the spring. They grow, flower, set seed and then die in the same season.

Half-Hardy Annuals HHA The seed of these plants will only germinate in warm conditions and the plants themselves will not withstand frost but they too grow and flower within a single season. Many of the subjects listed as HHA are actually perennial and will live from year to year if they are adequately protected during the winter.

Hardy Biennials HB These plants are invariably sown in the summer during which time they

Fig 47(b) Two-tone wallflower bed.

grow stems and leaves. They will live through the winter and then flower, after which they die. This category also contains many plants which are perennial but inferior performance in subsequent years does not merit their retention as permanent subjects.

Hardy Perennials HP Hardy perennials will live in the garden for many years. Most of them die down each winter and produce new stems and leaves in the following spring. However, there are many examples of evergreen perennials whose foliage is always present.

Half-Hardy Perennials HHP A half-hardy perennial is often a tropical or sub-tropical plant which will be killed by frost and consequently needs to be over-wintered in a greenhouse. Catalogues often classify these subjects as GP, or greenhouse perennials.

F_1 **Hybrids** A great many modern varieties are sold as F_1 Hybrids and they are produced by using two separate sets of inbred parent plants; one provides the pollen and the other produces the seed. Each successive batch of seed requires further parent plants to be raised with the same pollination procedures as before and the process is painstaking and laborious. This accounts for the fact that F_1 seed is very much more expensive, but the resulting plants are unusually vigorous, disease-resistant and very even in colour and form.

Open Pollinated Varieties The vast majority of seed is produced by growing the breeding plants in a field situation where they are pollinated by natural processes. The parent plants are selected and re-selected as an on-going process to ensure that the resultant offspring maintains the requisite characteristics.

51

CHAPTER 9

Spring Subjects

Alyssum saxatile HP

Most commonly grown in the rockery but it looks equally well in beds and is very reliable in any open situation. If it is retained as a permanent feature, it should be trimmed back after flowering to ensure compact growth. The varieties 'Golden Queen', 'Citrinum' and 'Gold Ball' are differing shades of yellow all reaching 9–12in (22–30cm) but the species *A. montanum* is a miniature, never reaching more than 4in (10cm).

Arabis (Rock Cress) HP

A lovely carpeting plant with typically white flowers in profusion but there are also pinks which can be grown from seed. The plant's height is between 4–8in (10–20cm) and the habit is spreading – inclining towards invasiveness – so it will need cutting back after a year or two.

Aubretia HP

Another flower which is principally used as a rockery subject to utilize its cascading habit. It is also a superb bedder, reaching only 3–4in (8–10cm). The colours range through reds, purple and various shades of blue and the seed is most often sold as a mixture such as 'Bengal' and 'Monarch'. However, there are separate colours available like 'Ruby Cascade' and 'Blue Cascade' and there is an F_1 hybrid called 'Novalis Blue'.

Auricula HP

These are fleshy-leaved members of the primrose family which have truly exquisite

Fig 48   Alyssum saxatile is suitable for herbaceous borders and rock gardens.

Fig 49   Aubretia makes a colourful show on rock banks or in a sunny position on rock gardens.

blooms in a wide range of colours. The plants are quite compact and well behaved and although not noted for mass impact, they make delightful edging or front of border subjects. Choice of varieties is very limited but most seed companies do offer a seed mixture.

Bellis perennis (Daisy)   HB

This is not the daisy which grows so well in lawns but it is closely related. Cultivated varieties are in various shades of red and pink or white and the flowers are either single or double. 'Pomponette' bears button-sized blooms and the 'Carpet' series is in three separate colours plus a mixture called 'Bright Carpet'; all of these are 4–6in (10–15cm) tall with 1in (2½cm) diameter flowers. The Royal Horticultural Society (RHS) award winner, 'Radar Red', has much larger flowers and so too has the 'Goliath Mixture'; the 'Super Monstrosa' strain – in three separate colours and a mixture – bears mostly double and large flowers. Choice plants can be divided after flowering and grown on for the following year because these daisies are perennials.

Forget-Me-Not (Myosotis)   HB

Few gardeners can forget this plant because it successfully propagates itself over most suburban areas but often as rather inferior examples of the species. 'Blue Ball', 'Miniature Blue' and 'Dwarf Royal Blue' are all compact, 6–8in (15–20cm), with fairly dense flower clusters and are excellent for edging.

'Blue Bird', 'Blue Cloud' and the larger 'Royal Blue' are 12in (30cm) high with loose sprays of blooms. The less compact varieties make good close companions for tulips and will sit happily in the light shade of taller subjects like wallflowers. You may also find the pink or white forget-me-nots very appealing.

Pansy   HA,HB,HP

The distinction between pansies and violas is not very clear as you will see if you look through a few catalogues but there is no point in confusing the issue even further. If we say that violas have

Fig 50   Bellis perennis *is amongst the most welcome of flowers, coming as it does in mid-spring and lasting until the summer bedding is ready to plant.*

smaller flowers, are more compact and are more perennial in their nature it won't please the botanists but it might be helpful. If you treat pansies as hardy biennials and sow them in early summer, they will start flowering in the following spring and continue to do so through summer. There are also some varieties which will flower during the winter when the weather is reasonable but their main display occurs in the spring. The F_1 'Universals' are the best known, followed by the 'Ultima' range which comprises twenty-two colours. The cheaper alternatives, however, are 'Floral Dance' and 'Gypsy Dance'.

Pansies are amongst the most popular of garden plants and you will find that most catalogues contain dozens of different varieties in a tremendous colour range and with many varied patterns. The winter-flowering types which I have mentioned do not have especially large flowers and if this is one of your requirements you should look at F_1s like the 'Majestic Giants' and 'Premier' and the long-standing favourites such as the 'Swiss Giants' and 'Roggli Giants'.

53

Fig 51 White polyanthus from the range of the 'Crescendo' series. It flowers throughout a mild winter and reaches its peak in spring.

Fig 52 Primulas are an essential part of the spring display but it is important to ensure that plants are grown or purchased which are suitable for outdoors.

Polyanthus   HP

Most catalogues offer a choice of F_1 hybrids and open pollinated strains of this plant but two varieties have dominated the scene for some years, namely the 'Pacific Giants' and 'Crescendo'. The latter is an F_1 hybrid and is exceptionally reliable and hardy, a favourite with parks' departments and one of the 'greats' of bedding. The colour range is wide and even in winter, the large heads of flowers are regularly seen. The 'Pacific Giants' and some other varieties are excellent in milder districts and their occasional winter flowers build to a climax in the spring.

Polyanthus seed is very small and germinates slowly and erratically but once you have the plants, they are undemanding except that they prefer moist soil and the shade of other plants during the summer. The plants are easily propagated by dividing them in the early summer.

Primula (Primrose)   HP

This huge group of plants, which includes the auricula and the polyanthus, has much to offer in the spring and the common primrose *P. vulgaris* should be in every garden. Unfortunately, many of the catalogue varieties have been bred for pots and are not winter-hardy. They are beautiful flowers but you will find, as I have, that they are unreliable in the garden. There is one fairly recent variety, however, called 'Husky', which has been specially bred for outdoor planting. Some of the laced varieties, whose petals are edged in a contrasting colour, are well worth trying; 'Asteroid' and 'Lace Maroon' are examples. The Wanda hybrids are lovely primroses, mostly very compact, very early in flower and completely hardy.

Two other primulas with different flower forms are also very desirable − *P. denticulata*, the 'Drumstick Primrose', in blues or white and the unusual 'candelabras' with their tiered clusters of flowers. *P. japonica*, *P. pulverulenta* and *P. beesiana* are all examples which also differ from the normal primrose in that their height reaches about 18in (45cm).

Fig 53(a) Primula denticulata – *suitable for spring bedding.*

If ever you want to explore a relatively untapped source of pleasure in gardening, I recommend that you try some of the dozens of uncommon primulas. The only real snag with the whole primrose family is that the seed is tricky to germinate, the most vital factor being that the very fine seed is sown on the surface of the compost which must never be allowed to dry out. A temperature of 55–60°F (13–16°C) is required and germination will be impaired if temperatures are consistently higher. Containers should therefore be placed in a cool place out of reach of direct sunshine.

Stocks (Matthiola)   HB

Changing fashions have left the stocks rather neglected as a garden plant but they are still seen as cut flowers and very pretty they are. It is the

Brompton stocks which are specially for spring bedding but the East Lothians can also be used both as biennials and annuals. Unfortunately, although both are listed as hardy plants, they suffer badly during winter months and really need to be protected in a frame or cold greenhouse. This extra chore has reduced stocks to rarities in spring displays, except in mild areas, and their lovely fragrance is sadly missed. Most catalogues offer no choice at all, only a mixture which includes single and double flowers but in quite a large colour range.

Sweet-William (*Dianthus barbatus*)   HB

The lovely clusters of scented flower-heads suggest another age of gardening as these plants too have suffered a loss of popularity, perhaps because they flower later than most spring subjects and may be considered obstacles to the planting of summer bedding. Nonetheless, they are a joy and the seed companies have at least half a dozen strains from which to select and you will notice some varieties which can be grown as annuals to flower in mid-summer.

The auricula-eyed varieties are charming and mostly 18–24in (45–60cm) tall but there are some splendid dwarf strains, such as 'Indian Carpet', which are only half that height. Perhaps I should emphasize that in colder districts, sweet-williams should not be considered as spring subjects because their flowering will probably coincide with early summer.

Wallflowers (Cheiranthus)   HB

The backbone of many spring bedding displays, wallflowers can be a disappointment in severe winters and can be disastrous if the clubroot disease is present in the soil, but their super qualities of scent and colour make ample compensation. The catalogues offer a wide variety of seeds from the taller ones like 'Cloth of Gold' and 'Fair Lady' at 15–18in (35–45cm) to the Bedder series at 12in (30cm) and the dwarf strain, 'Tom Thumb', which produces plants 6–9in (15–22cm) tall. You will also come across *C. allionii*, the Siberian wallflower, which will flower

Fig 53(b)   Pansies in stagger pots, ready for planting out.

rather later than the other; it is sometimes listed as Erysimum.

One thing which I would recommend, is the use of at least some of the single colour varieties. Spring gardens usually have a wide range of colours from other subjects and a long-flowering plant like the wallflower will offer a confused scene if only the mixtures are used.

Plants are often purchased for planting out in the autumn and the quality is sometimes deplorable. Wallflowers are often field-grown and merely uprooted to be offered for sale and these quite large plants have little chance of becoming sufficiently well established to cope with a severe winter. Container plants are an option but I believe that raising wallflowers from seed is by far the most satisfactory way of achieving a good show. The plants are grown during the summer months and need neither artificial heat, nor the shelter of a greenhouse – home-grown is definitely best.

Viola (Violet)   HB,HP

Adopting the view that violas are small pansies, they make marvellous subjects for spring and there is an impressive selection of varieties offered as seed. They are mostly in mixtures such as the 'Little Face' types like 'Bambini' and 'Funny Face' but there are separate colours like 'Prince Henry' which is deep purple; 'Yellow Prince' is a deep yellow and 'Chantreyland' has a rich apricot colouring.

CHAPTER 10

Summer Plants: The Magnificent Seven

We all have favourite plants and, naturally, they are the ones which should be given pride of place but, regardless of personal preferences, there are some summer subjects which have all the requisite virtues:

(i)   Long lasting performance
(ii) Colour impact, or 'flower power'
(iii) Resistance to adverse weather

All the plants listed in this chapter possess these characteristics to a greater or lesser extent, which means that any gardener who wants a trouble-free and colourful display, without the fuss of choosing from hundreds of candidates, can select any or all of these 'Magnificent Seven'. There is sufficient variation in colour and form to allow for a variety of tastes; all these plants are continuous-flowering and even the most suspect of them shows good resilience against wet or dry weather. Only one decision has to be made – do you actually like them?

Begonia semperflorens   HHA
(Fibrous-rooted Begonia)

This is the supreme edging and dwarf bedding plant – compact, drought-resistant, tolerant of shade, happy in the sun and it flowers until the first real frost. Even in a very wet summer, the flowering performance is excellent and the leaves, which are shiny and either green or bronze, are always attractive.

There are many varieties available and most of them are F_1 hybrids but they can be conveniently

Fig 54 A raised display next to the Colegrave offices near Banbury in Oxfordshire. Red and Rose Begonia semperflorens *in harmony with* Cineraria 'Silver Dust'.

listed under two main groupings. The traditional ones are 6–8in (15–20cm) tall and include 'Lucia', 'Organdy', 'Cocktail', 'Coco', 'Royale' and the 'Devil' series. They are usually sold as mixtures in terms of both flower and foliage colour, but single colours are available.

The intermediate group contains fewer varieties and so far these larger plants have not achieved the popularity of the former group, except perhaps in parks' displays where the larger flower-size is useful. Some intermediates are 'Wings', 'Danica' and 'Fortuna' and perhaps the 'Olympic' series should be included because, although the plants are smaller, their flowers are equally large.

Perhaps the only limitation of these begonias is the rather restricted colour range which only extends to a few reds, various shades of pink, and white. However, this limitation does mean that the various mixtures of flower and foliage hues do blend very well together and this is not true of some other bedding subjects.

Neither the All American Selections (AAS) nor Fleuroselect have honoured a *B. semperflorens* but some have received RHS awards, including 'Coco Ducolour', 'Athena' and 'Stara Deep Rose'; 'Stara Rose' and 'Stara White' were given the coveted Springfields Certificate of Outstanding Performance (SCOOP) award in 1987. Strangely, even some of the prizewinners are dropped from catalogues because new varieties of begonias along with several other flowers are introduced with amazing regularity. Often, the new varieties gain favour with commercial growers, who are the biggest customers, simply because they may flower slightly earlier. This gives the grower a trading advantage but is of no real benefit to you, the domestic gardener and of course, new varieties cost more than old ones.

The seed of these begonias is expensive as most F_1 hybrid seed is, but you may wish to try the cheaper alternatives such as 'Summer Rainbow' and 'Options' and these will be perfectly satisfactory in small groups. If you are planning a large display, however, I advise you to use the F_1 plants because the others will be far too variable in height, habit and performance.

It can be an economic proposition to grow begonias from seed because the ready-to-plant purchase will be very expensive and reflects the fact that four or five months can be needed between germination and the mature plant. But the seed is difficult to handle and the slow-growing seedlings may present problems. Professional growers invariably use artificial light and higher temperatures than would be normal in an amateur greenhouse but success can be achieved, with care, under glass and on the window-sill.

Begonia (Tuberous-rooted Begonia)   HHP

If I were faced by the 'desert island' plant dilemma, this is definitely the one I would choose to take with me; I am sure that it is the most effective bedding plant of all. It comfortably satisfies the requirement for a prolonged display, the foliage makes an admirable foil to the spectacular blooms – which are fully double and in a rich range of colours, dark and light pinks, reds and scarlets, orange, white and a really beautiful apricot.

These begonias can be bought as tubers but the colour range which I have just described is that of a series which is grown from seed, known as 'Non Stop'. This has been the premier variety for some years and has resisted the challenge from 'Musical', 'Memory', 'Clips' and the most recent newcomer to date, 'Spirit' (which was brought out in 1990). Also in that year, 'Elatior' which had been a very successful house-plant, became available from seed and proved its value as a bedding plant.

Seed for the tuberous begonia is even costlier than for *B. semperflorens* and the problems of raising the plants is somewhat greater because the seedlings must receive more than twelve hours a day sunlight in order to make top growth. This means that supplementary light is required unless sowing is delayed until March and the consequence will be plants which will not flower until at least mid-July. The good news is that if you do raise plants from seed or buy them as green plants, the tubers can be lifted at the end of the season and stored until the next year. If the tubers are then started into growth early in spring, cuttings can be taken and you will quickly have a most desirable collection.

Tuberous begonias are less enthusiastic about dry weather conditions than their fibrous relatives and a moisture-retentive soil will encourage the best results. I well remember seeing a major display in Torquay during the drought of 1989. The display was well below par because of the lack of rainfall and the water restrictions.

Fig 55   Begonia 'Light Pink Devil' with its bronze foliage looks excellent in
any company; seen here with rudbeckia and African marigolds.

Busy Lizzie (Impatiens)   HHA

As a house-plant, the Busy Lizzie was admired as much for its strength of character as for its beauty but since the plant breeders gave it so much attention, it has become a formidable garden plant. It has been the most popular bedding subject in the US for some years and will soon achieve that status in the UK and every other garden-conscious country. Its principal qualities are tremendous flowering capacity, good wet weather tolerance, compact growth habit and the fact that it is the best bedding subject for flowering in shade – its colour range is also unequalled. Its performance is impaired by drought conditions especially if the plants have not established themselves before the dryness becomes severe. It could be argued that the foliage of impatiens is bland but this is perhaps appropriate when there is so much bloom.

The dominant varieties over the recent years have been 'Accent' – with its large flowers in a range of eighteen colours – and 'Super Elfin' which has smaller flowers but a more uniform habit. 'Novette', also known as 'Florette', has also been a remarkable series and so too have the 'Sparkles' which are called 'Twinkles' outside Europe. The 'Starbright' variety has flowers with a central white star pattern and 'Blitz Orange' and 'Blitz Violet' have a more upright and vigorous habit with blooms which can be 2in (5cm) in diameter. Varieties like 'Cleopatra', 'Confection' and 'Rosette' are unusual in that they have double and semi-double blooms.

As with most bedding plants, the most popular

Fig 56 Begonia 'Non Stop' has proved
immensely – and repeatedly – popular. It is
grown from seed, but the results are worth
the extra effort.

impatiens are the mixtures but it should be
realised that the growth habits of different-
coloured plants within the mix do vary slightly –
but on average, they are 9in (22cm) tall. The huge
number of varieties of some subjects can be
bewildering and this is certainly true of Busy Lizzies. Different plant breeders produce new
strains independently and give them appealing
names but most gardeners would find it nearly
impossible to distinguish between them.
However, you are unlikely to be disappointed
with any of the varieties which I have mentioned
and I am sure that you will be captivated by the
newer pastel shades which are emerging.

The Busy Lizzie, just like the begonias, is peren-

nial by nature and any especially attractive plants
in the display can be potted up before the heavy
frosts begin, and kept in the greenhouse or
home. In spring, cuttings can be taken but you
may find that the resultant plants will not be
identical in habit of growth, although flower colour and size will usually be the same.

Growing these plants from seed is not so difficult as begonias but success is not certain
because the seedlings are sometimes awkward if
the conditions are not quite right. The best
results are achieved by delaying sowing until late
March or early April when the natural light levels
have improved and optimum temperatures are
more easily maintained. Impatiens begin flowering whilst they are quite small and the disadvantages of a later start are hardly evident.

The 'New Guinea' hybrid impatiens have been
around for some years as pot plants, combining
the dual appeal of large flowers and interesting,
often variegated leaves. The first introductions
were propagated vegetatively but then
'Tangeglow' and 'Sweet Sue' arrived – both
grown from seed but neither having distinguished
foliage. 'Tango', with its huge, orange flowers,
came on the scene in 1989 and in the same year
there were other newcomers of the same type –
the 'Bull' and 'Kientzler' series bred in Germany
and the 'Celebrations' which were produced in
Costa Rica. Some of these have bronzy-green
leaves but of the Kientzlers, a variety called 'Epia'
bears foliage which develops variegations as it

Fig 57 Even a large container can be used for
a single subject planting; in this case, a 'New
Guinea' hybrid impatiens.

Fig 58 Impatiens are destined to become the first choice summer flower for beds, baskets and virtually every other situation around the garden.

matures. On the other hand, the Celebrations are notable for yellow variegations, particularly on the varieties 'Carousel', 'Champions', 'Jubilee' and 'Parade'.

The newer 'New Guineas' will gradually become more widespread amongst the seed catalogues but if you are impatient to try them, you will have to buy potted plants which will be quite expensive. However, you will quickly build up your stocks because they are extremely eager to root as cuttings, taken in late spring or throughout the summer. I am convinced that the 'New Guineas' will become immensely popular for summer bedding not just because of their foliage characteristics but also as Busy Lizzies which look entirely different to their multiflora relatives.

French Marigold (*Tagetes patula*)   HHA
Marigold is a confusing category because of the large number of different plants which the word covers and the variability of the other descriptive words. Most come under the generic heading of *Tagetes* but this is usually used for the smaller, single-flowered marigolds. Another main group is

the Africans, often called Americans, which are taller and with large globular blooms; the titles are misleading because the plant originates in Mexico. Then there are the Afro-French and pot marigolds, also called calendula. The French marigolds are dwarf plants which are further divided into flowering types – crested, single and carnation-flowered. It is very bewildering but once you have sorted it out, you will discover really remarkable bedding plants.

The magic of marigolds is that they produce a profusion of gorgeous blooms which deserve more appreciation than they usually get. The French types begin flowering within five or six weeks of sowing the seed and continue until the frosts arrive and the growth remains compact and tidy – most are between 6–12in (15–30cm). There are dozens of varieties in the catalogues, all superb, in a colour range from yellow, through gold, to red, to a rich brown which is sometimes called mahogany. It is rather churlish to select from them but my own favourites are the double-flowered 'Boy', 'Hero', 'Aurora' and 'Alamo' series and one named 'Queen Bee'. The Afro-French marigolds bear even larger flowers but the plants are very compact and do not set seed. Unable to fulfil its primary function, the plant has more energy to devote to flowering and the display retains its youthful appearance. The 'Fireworks' and 'Solar' series are outstandding and I particularly like the variety 'Red Seven Star'.

It is good news that the seed is large and easily managed; it germinates within days at around 70°F (20°C) and the seedlings are sturdy and quick-growing. This means that sowing can be left until late April but be warned, these marigolds are very tender and the hardening-off process should be gradual otherwise the plants will sustain damage.

Geranium (Zonal Pelargonium)   HHP
By now, we all know that geraniums should be called perlargoniums and we are also aware that the seed and the plants are the most expensive of any used for bedding. At one time, only cut-

Fig 59 Two of the most successful bedding plants —geranium 'Century Scarlet' and impatiens 'Accent Mixed'.

Fig 60 There are dozens of different hybrid geraniums but this one called 'Hollywood Star' is distinct from all the others.

tings were grown but now there are many hybrids which can be grown very easily. Unfortunately, many of the most common of these new varieties were very disappointing, although there are dozens which perform exceedingly well.

Few plants are able to withstand dry conditions like geraniums can and they are at their best when rainfall is sparse and sunshine is plentiful but the best varieties will put on a reasonable show even in cool, damp summers. Whether the seed-raised plants are better than the established named varieties is still debated but, like it or not, the F_1 hybrids rule the roost. The only way to get favourite cultivars like 'Paul Crampel' and 'Caroline Schmidt' is to deal with the specialist nurseries and, thereafter, you will need to take cuttings to increase your stock. It is certainly true that the hybrids do not have the characteristics of the old cultivars because there are very few with double flowers and none at all with ornamental foliage like the beautiful 'Mrs Henry Cox'. Geranium enthusiasts will also argue that the seed hybrids are coarse plants and that their flowers lack refinement.

The F_1 hybrids have been bred for uniformity of habit and regular flowers, and the colour range is now quite extensive. One problem remains, however, seed which is sown in the greenhouse in January will not usually result in flowering plants before the end of June. Those who buy plants in May will almost certainly be getting geraniums which have been 'forced' in warm conditions and treated with chemicals which hurry the flowers along and yet keep the plants compact.

Whatever criticism is levelled at the hybrid geraniums, it cannot be denied that the gardening public are pleased with the results of their purchases and the better varieties do give excellent displays in parks and gardens everywhere. Greenhouse owners who sow the seed in November and over-winter the seedlings at 41–45°F (5–7°C) will have plants in bud at the right time for bedding out. The young plants should be encouraged to become dormant and this entails allowing the compost to dry out until such time as natural conditions are conducive to continued growth.

Of the earliest varieties, 'Sprinter' is still sold and so too are a couple of the 'Diamond' series which won Fleuroselect awards – 'Scarlet Diamond' and 'Cherry Diamond'. The highly rated 'Gala' varieties are still offered, mostly as a mixture, but the present state of the art is widely thought to be the 'Century' geraniums which are available in more than a dozen separate colours. Two new geraniums were presented to the public in 1990 with a huge amount of publicity and hailed as a major advance. They were the achievements of two different plant breeders who came up with similar results and were described by one breeder as floribunda and by the other as multibloom. Neither has the rounded flower-heads of other geraniums, they are flatter and contain fewer florets, but they can produce ten or more flower stems at one time and the mass colour effect is impressive. Both the 'Sensation floribunda' and the 'Multiblooms' tend to reach the flowering stage about two weeks earlier than the other F_1 hybrids, and this may be the most important factor for amateur growers.

Geraniums receive a great deal of attention from breeders because they are commercially successful plants and there is no doubt that new varieties will emerge almost every year. You may reach the conclusion that, for garden purposes, there is little to choose from the myriad varieties and therefore you should select your colours and be prepared to try one of the major series each year.

Pansy   HP

Traditionalists do not embrace the pansy as a summer plant, thinking that it should have remained very much in its natural spring period but now, as I pointed out in the previous chapter, there are varieties which can flower in every month of the year if conditions are favourable. The 'Universals', which as the advertising says is 'the only pansy that's asked for by name' has been bred for winter and spring display but it

Fig 61 The 'Jolly Joker' pansy is certainly an unusual combination of colours and is likely to become a garden favourite.

must be said that they will perform in the summer as well. Naturally they do not compare with the quality of the American-bred 'Majestic Giants' or the famous 'Swiss' types which are still produced by Roggli in Switzerland. The 'Imperial' strain from Japan is rightly popular for 'Imperial Orange', 'Imperial Silver Princess' and the 'Antique Shades' which are in delicate pastel colours. The 'Clear Crystals' are sold in individual colours but with smaller flowers than the others so far mentioned and a variety called 'Azure Blue' is the brightest blue in the whole pansy kingdom. 'Brunig' is a rich mahogany colour with a thin gold edge around each petal and what can I say about 'Jolly Joker'? A multi prize-winner in

1990, its unique combination of purple upper petals and bright orange lower petals is greatly admired – and despised!

Having accomplished the major task of choosing your pansies for the season, it is reassuring to know that the seed germinates readily and the plants are easily grown on to the planting stage without the need for much additional heat. Dead-heading will prolong the summer display but you can also grow some later plants which will invigorate the show when the earlier pansies are beginning to fade. If some plants have grown quite large, they will benefit from being cut down to about 3in (8cm) from the base so that new shoots will be prompted. Pansies do suffer from a fungal disease which builds up in the soil and is simply called pansy sickness and this may become apparent if they are continually grown in the same patch of ground. Watering with a copper-based fungicide should control the problem but you would be advised to plant elsewhere in successive seasons.

Petunia   HHA

Of the three main types which are sold, the double and grandifloras have very big flowers and are more suited to sheltered containers and hanging baskets. The multifloras have been bred for open garden situations and their flowers, though still quite large, are more resilient and rain-resistant despite the fact that most petunias have been bred in California. The colours are breath-taking and range from pastel shades to vivid purples and reds, and there are many novelties with white edges and stars – as well as those whose petals show some dramatic veining. For some gardens, the stronger colours are too powerful and should be planted in moderation. One catalogue described petunias as 'the most stunning bedding plants in the world' and in a dry, sunny year, that description is apt. Although the texture of the flowers seems fragile, they are capable of surprising recovery after rain. The succession of blooms is so regular that any damage is not apparent for long.

'Dwarf Resisto' was the outstanding variety for

Fig 62(a)   The petunia is certainly one of the most glamorous flowers and the range of colours is enormous. 'Frenzy Orchid' is one of the newer ones.

many years and is still available in at least some of the original colours and in mixture. 'Frenzy' is a more recent variety and boasts about ten separate colours, most of them with veined petals which strengthen the flowers as well as looking distinctive. 'Starship' is a series with mostly striped blooms and if you must have yellow, which is the rarest petunia colour, the 'Brass Band' mixture contains some primrose-coloured flowers.

Petunias flower close to the top of the shoots and these extend through the season, becoming longer and somewhat naked below. This can be disguised by pinching some stems in mid-summer and also by using more compact plants of other kinds to cover the bareness.

Fig 62(b)   An unusual hanging basket made up of Petunia 'Frenzy Pink'.

Reprise on the Magnificent Seven

With the exception of pansies, these plants are tender and whether bought from shops or raised from seed, the process of hardening off is vital to avoid either damage or the disappointment of poor performance. They are all perennial, they make good pot plants and will survive as such if they are protected during the winter. Each of them can be propagated from cuttings so that the colours which you have enjoyed most can be selected for preservation and you can build a collection for future seasons – with the exception of French marigolds which should be thrown away.

If you decide to leave pansies in the garden, you will find that their quality deteriorates over the years, but if you take cuttings, the plants will have a new lease of life. Seedlings will also naturally result from your plants, but if they are F_1 hybrids, the offspring will usually be decidedly inferior. However, the seed harvested from open pollinated varieties will produce plants which are similar to the parents and you may wish to grow them and select the best ones for future use.

None of the 'Magnificent Seven' is a perfect bedding plant but each one tries very hard and you will not find a 'baddie' among them.

CHAPTER 11

Summer Plants: Best of the Rest

This chapter is devoted to those bedding plants which have excellent characteristics but, sometimes by a small margin, fail to match the qualities of the 'Magnificent Seven'. Some are garden favourites of long standing and we would not wish to exclude them just because they fail to meet the most stringent requirements of performance, longevity, weather resistance or colour impact. In fact, some are of special interest simply because they are not high impact plants and are useful for their more subtle qualities. In the future, it may be that breeders will be able to correct some of the deficiencies and new strains of these plants will take their place amongst the very best.

African Marigolds (*Tagetes erecta*)   HHA

Big, bold, and some might say vulgar, are words that might be used to describe these dominant plants. At one time, they were all 2–3ft (60–90cm) tall but breeders have sought to reduce their height whilst maintaining their flower size – and they have succeeded. My reservation about these marigolds is that a plant which is 1ft (30cm) high should not have blooms which are 4in (10cm) across. Of course, if they are grown together in a bed, my complaint is somewhat negated but the largest flowers do seem out of scale. A less subjective objection concerns the stems which, especially on later flowers, are unable to hold the blooms erect either because of wind or because of the extra weight of a soggy flower head. Dead-heading is imperative to avoid the eyesore of a mass of decaying petals and also to remove a regular source of mould. Lest you think me unduly critical of the African giants, I must say that their impact *en masse* is matched by very few other subjects.

As I write this, I am looking at a group in my own garden which reminds me of the dangers of buying mixed seed for small displays. My plants are the 'Perfection' series which includes gold, orange and yellow and of the dozen which I planted, nine are yellow, two are orange and the other one is gold! They are 12–18in (30–45cm) tall which is slightly taller than a similar series of African pygmies called the 'Incas'; both strains provide power without finesse but the individual blooms are stupendous. The 'Lady' series has been around for many years and I regard 'Primrose Lady' as the finest colour amongst African marigolds. There are also the real giants like 'Doubloon', 'Treasure Trove', 'Climax' and 'Gold Coin' which will normally attain 3ft (90cm) but these appear to be dying breeds.

Just like their French brothers, African marigolds are almost instant from seed – just sow and stand back – but they are equally prone to set-backs from low temperatures and should be hardened off carefully.

Ageratum (Floss Flower)   HHA

The blue varieties of this fluffy-flowering edging plant are justifiably popular but very few people seem to grow the pink or white ones. Perhaps this is because the dead flowers of ageratum turn brown and it looks particularly disagreeable with

Fig 63 The high impact colours of 'Perfection' African marigolds are balanced by the subtle hues of rudbeckia 'Rustic Dwarfs'.

the lighter colours. The flower-heads are difficult to remove and it would be a dedicated gardener who would attempt thorough dead-heading of these plants. If ageratum does decline rather prematurely, it is possible to rejuvenate the display by using scissors but in a summer with normal rainfall, the duration of bloom is quite satisfactory.

'Blue Mink' is the most common variety but it is decidedly inferior to 'Blue Champion' – also known as 'Blue Danube' – which is an F_1 hybrid and the extra cost of the seed is definitely worth-while. Also notable is the 'Ocean' series bred in Holland which includes 'Adriatic', 'Atlantic' and 'Pacific' which exist in various shades of blue or purple. You may also find the bi-coloured varieties 'Southern Cross' and 'Capri' to be an interesting alternative to the uniform shades of

the others. It is also worth knowing that there are varieties such as 'Blue Bouquet' which are much taller than the edging types and make an excellent 'dot' plant and useful cut flower. They are 18in (45cm) high whereas the 'edgers' are 8in (20cm) tall.

Alyssum (Sweet Alyssum) HA

This sweet-smelling hardy annual is an ever-present in many gardens but it is not without its problems. Alyssum is prone to mildew as a seed-ling when it is grown too wet and as a mature plant in hot summers. It can also become the ghost of its former self in very dry periods, especially when its position puts it in competition with more capable plants, and it is always worth sowing a later batch of seed for replacements. Another irritating difficulty is that some of the older varieties like 'Carpet of Snow' may vary in flowering and growth habit depending on where you buy the seed from. Seed producers need vigilance to maintain the quality of their strains and perhaps 'Carpet of Snow' has suffered some neglect. if alyssum is well grown and kept moist, it should remain low and floriferous for most of the summer.

'Snow Crystals' is the best white. It has larger flowers than other types whilst retaining a neat mounded habit and, although it is a triploid and thus sets no seed, it is not much more expensive to buy. 'Morning Mist', 'Magic Circle' and 'Pastel Carpet' are good mixtures containing pinks, purples, whites and creams and if you want something different, 'Oriental Night' is a strong purple.

Antirrhinum (Snapdragon)   HHA,HA

The dear old snapdragon was a great favourite of the Victorians and is still going fairly strong with its several flowering types which are described as azalea, hyacinth, penstemon and butterfly. Unfortunately, antirrhinums are susceptible to a disease called rust which is prevalent in some parts of Britain and America, from where it originates, and the results can be devastating. There are a few rust-resistant varieties and these should be grown if the disease threatens.

Of the taller varieties, 'Madame Butterfly' at 30in (75cm) and the slightly shorter 'Coronettes', have led the field but the shorter plants are increasingly favoured. 'Floral Carpet', 'Pixie' and the 'Impact' series – all F_1 hybrids – are 10–15in (25–35cm) but 'Cheerio' and 'Magic Carpet' are

Fig 64 The author's garden. One part of it is entirely devoted to summer bedding plants, and is shown here just after planting out in the first week of June.

good open pollinated plants, the latter being a real dwarf at just 6in (15cm). There are, however, numerous alternatives to those mentioned and there is little difference in their garden performance. You may also want to choose one of the single colour strains although, at present, not many are offered.

Seed must be sown early in the year but the seedlings are practically hardy and should be grown as cool as possible to produce sturdy plants. It is perhaps advisable to pinch out the growing tips when about 3in (8cm) has been reached so that your antirrhinums are bushy but, otherwise, they are not choosy about soil or position and the results are quite good even in partial shade. A question mark hangs over the continuity of flowering and the first spikes must

be removed as soon as the petals have fallen to ensure a further flush of blooms.

Aster (Callistephus)   HHA

Asters start flowering rather later than most summer subjects but this drawback apart, they are marvellous bedding plants. They are prone to a wicked disease called wilt – which is a soil-borne ailment with fearsome results – but most gardeners will not see the disease. Asters come long and short, in an impressive colour range and also with differing forms of flowers. The tall 'Duchess' plants at 24in (60cm) and the slightly shorter 'Ostrich Plumes' will add height to any display and their blooms are of the highest quality. The 'Rivieras' have very large and fully double flowers, the 'Milady' series – which are available

Fig 65   Same view of the same bed but six weeks later showing rudbeckia, African marigolds, French marigolds, antirrhinums, Begonia semperflorens, nicotiana and mixed impatiens.

Fig 66 The 'Duchess' strain of asters has been popular for many years and although they come in bloom rather late, they remain colourful well into the autumn.

Carnations (Dianthus)   HHA

Sadly, carnations have become rare in domestic and public displays and this may be due to the rather sloppy habit of the long-standing varieties. The modern plants are greatly improved in this respect and the 'Lillipot' and 'Knight' series are probably the pick of the bunch, the former is about 6in (15cm) and the latter 10in (25cm) high. Both are completely self-supporting with sturdy stems and good flowers but neither is especially fragrant. They are both very good for pots but in the garden you will find a large number of buds which fail to develop – this doesn't detract from the impact of the display, however. 'Dwarf Fragrance' is an aptly named mixture but it will not give the mass effect of Lillipot and the

hormone rooting powder

Fig 67 Cuttings – cut cleanly below a leaf node and remove the bottom leaf. Dip the cut end in rooting powder and insert in compost.

in three colours and a mixture – are 10–12in (25–30cm) tall and the 'Roundabout' strain produces slightly shorter dome-shaped plants. Although they have no resistance to wilt and have existed since the early 1970s, winning a Fleuroselect medal in 1974, the 'Pinocchios' are splendid. I believe they are amongst the most attractive bedding plants.

Mature plants are not so easily obtained and choice is limited but most of the seed catalogues have a large range on offer and sowing and growing is quite straightforward. Incidentally, the dwarf varieties make lovely pot plants.

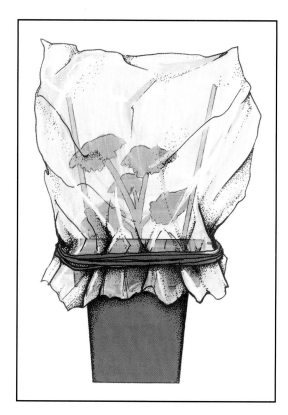

Fig 68   A propagating 'tent' made with sticks
and a plastic bag.

they too can be grown from seed and although
the resultant giants will be of varying quality, the
best ones can be saved for subsequent years.

The dwarf bedders are also variable but the
average height of 2ft (60cm) or less makes them
an admirable choice for general garden planting.
There is a wide range of colours in most of the
seed mixtures and there are a few in single
colours – red, pink and yellow – and others with
double flowers like their exhibition counterparts.
All dahlias make substantial plants and even the
dwarfs will have a spread of about 2ft (60cm).

The seed is inexpensive and germinates readily
and because they grow very quickly sowing can

Fig 69   There are many dahlias which grow
easily from seed but this 'Collarette Dandy' is
surely one of the most distinctive.

Knights. There are some novelties around too,
like 'King of the Blacks', 'Stripes and Picotees' and
'Black and White Minstrels'.

Carnations will not give a long display but their
'flower power' is good and they are excellent for
cutting. The varieties described are basically
annual in character but some will survive the
winter and, anyway, cuttings root easily and can
be protected if necessary.

Dahlia   HHP
Enthusiasts of these dazzling plants usually grow
named cultivars from tubers and cuttings which
reach 3–4ft (90–120cm) in height and require
substantial stakes to support them. A border of
these dahlias is a majestic sight with flowers
which can be in a variety of forms and as large as
10in (25cm) across but most gardeners will rather
consider the bedding dahlias grown from seed. If,
however, you want the giant exhibition types,

Fig 70 There is no denying that a large group of dahlias makes a spectacular sight, demonstrated here on Southport promenade.

'Redskin' is similar but with the added attraction of bronze leaves. The 'Sunny' series has mostly double flowers in separate colours but the plants are variable and the seed is expensive. Whatever variety you grow, these dahlias will flower continuously until the first frost and give ample supplies of cut blooms.

Gazania   HHA

These dramatically showy flowers are like technicolour daisies but they do have a slight deficiency — the flowers close up in the late afternoon and also when the weather is especially dull. When the sun shines, they look wonderful and their silvery-green foliage makes a pleasant background for the bright blooms. 'Colorama' and the 'Daybreak' group, which offers separate colours, are excellent and you will not be disappointed with the more widely available 'Chansonette' and 'Carnival' mixtures. 'Mini Star Tangerine' has been a European and American prize-winner and, more recently, the variety 'Garden Sun' won a Fleuroselect gold medal.

Gazanias are perennial but not winter-hardy and if you want to save any plants, they must be potted up and protected from frost. They are easily raised from seed, preferably sown in early spring, but in the mild districts they can be sown outside from late April.

Lobelia   HHA

Another extremely popular edging plant which will just about last in flower from the end of May until the frosts, especially in a good soil and with an adequate supply of moisture. Most gardeners grow lobelia for its blue shades but there are pinks, maroons, violets and white and a recent lilac-coloured introduction called 'Lavender Lady'. The blue varieties have almost become household names. The pale beauty of 'Cambridge Blue', the white-eyed, royal blue of 'Mrs Clibran' and 'Crystal Palace' whose deep blue looks 'electric' against the dark bronze foliage.

Lobelia seed is very small; it needs care to sow it evenly and the seedlings are tiny enough to present pricking out difficulties, but you will find

be left until late April. Don't forget that they are very tender subjects and must not be planted in the garden until the danger of frost is over. At the end of the season, if you so decide, the tubers can be dug up, cleaned and then stored in a frost-free situation until the following year.

Perhaps the most attractive and unusual flowers are those from a variety called 'Dandy', having single blooms with a 'collarette' or central collar of smaller petals in a contrasting colour. The most successful and long-standing dwarfs are the 'Coltness Hybrids' which are sold by most seed merchants; the plants are fairly uniform and the colour range is excellent. 'Rigoletto' bears semi-double blooms with differing shapes and but is still detectable in the evening and at night. The colour range is limited and the flowers look rather dull but they are produced abundantly over the whole season. I prefer them in small groups because the tubular part of the bloom is invariably horizontal and large groups give a jumbled impression. Seed is commonly sold as a mixture but it is possible to get separate colours and I think the lime green is the outstanding one. Germination is straightforward and the after-care of the young plants is uncomplicated.

Penstemon (Beard Tongue)   HP,HHA

Why this plant is not in every garden is a mystery

Fig 71   The most famous varieties of lobelia have existed for many years, including this one which has unusual bronze leaves and is called 'Crystal Palace'.

plenty in the packet for your money. The plants are slow-growing and you should aim to complete your sowings by the end of February or the beginning of March.

Nicotiana (Tobacco Plant)   HHA

The forerunners of the modern bedding nicotiana were tall and with flowers which closed during the day but the breeding work which was embarked upon has resulted in the 'Nicki' strain from America and the 'Domino' hybrids bred by Floranova in Britain. Both are about 12in (30cm) high with resilient flowers and succeed very well in bedding situations, often being the last subjects to be cut down by the frosts. In both strains, the characteristic tobacco plant scent has diminished

Fig 72   The 'Domino' series of nicotiana does not contain many colours but, like this red example, the low-key effect is most pleasant.

73

Fig 73 Penstemons are endearing flowers and although they are unreliable perennials, they are simple to grow, each year, as annuals.

annuals may survive the winter in soils which are well drained but all can be saved by potting them up for greenhouse protection and cuttings can be taken from favoured plants.

Pinks (Dianthus)   HHA,HP

Dianthus is the botanic category which includes carnations and pinks but the latter are much more inclined towards being perennials that the carnations which were described earlier. The modern pinks have Chinese ancestry and many of the recent introductions can be traced to the Heddewigii strains or those developed by the British firm of Allwood. They are outstanding for the size and quality of bloom, together with a compact and tidy habit but, like the carnations, they cannot be described as continuous flowering.

'Telstar' is a Fleuroselect winner of some years standing and also of special merit are 'Magic Charms', 'Fire Carpet', 'Brilliancy' and 'Snowfire', most of which are sweetly fragrant. The seed of pinks is quite large and the germination and after-care are without problems. Most pinks are 12in (30cm) or less in height.

Portulaca (Sun Plant)   HHA

A most striking flower in vivid colours which is somewhat similar to those of shrub roses but this plant is almost ignored by the gardening fraternity. This may be because the species refuses to open its flowers except in sunshine but breeders have reduced this tendency and the new strains like 'Sundial', 'Bloom Long' and 'Sunnyside' are much improved in this respect and the 'Extra' series, in separate colours, is likewise well-behaved. Another variety called 'Cloudbeater' highlights the problem and overcomes it with sparkling reds, pinks, white and a lovely shade of apricot. I think it is likely that portulaca will become an established favourite before very long, combining the merits of perpetual flowering and a very compact habit − 4−6in (10−15cm).

Rudbeckia   HHA

These easily grown and beautiful flowers are

to me but it has received scant attention from breeders and is not greatly publicized by the seed companies. It is a truly exquisite flower − reminiscent of the foxglove − which is unreliably hardy, but the annual varieties are entirely satisfactory. Most catalogues list at least one mixture, of which 'Bouquet' and 'Skyline' are examples and one called 'True Blue' is the only separate coloured strain of which I am aware. 'Skyline' is also known as 'Hyacinth Flowered' and was the subject of an Award of Merit after trials at the RHS gounds in Wisley. Some plants, like the fox-glove, produce stems which bear flowers on one side only but many have them all around.

Even those varieties which are described as

Fig 74 *Rudbeckia 'Rustic Dwarfs' have a superb 'warm' colouring which make them compatible with most other subjects. They make lovely cut flowers.*

early sowings but otherwise March is the favoured month. Incidentally, there is an alternative to yellows and browns with a dark pink rudbeckia called 'Brilliant' but this reaches 4ft (120cm) and some support is advisable.

Sweet peas (Lathyrus)   HA

These wonderful flowers are enormously popular and it is likely that gardeners spend more money on sweet pea seeds than any other. it is a plant which should be in the 'magnificent' group but the limitations – which are sometimes imagined – do stop many people from growing them. The basic problem is that they need support – or at least most of them do – hedges are

Fig 75 *By providing invisible means of support – stakes and string or netting – sweet peas can be featured in beds, as here at Harlow Car Gardens.*

ideal for adding that little extra to a summer bedding show. The three most prominent varieties were bred by Hurst in Britain – 'Rustic Dwarfs' sport richly coloured blooms in shades of gold and brown; 'Marmalade' has golden yellow flowers and 'Goldilocks' is semi-double, also in yellow shades. The flowers are large and daisy-like with dark central cones and they are very attractive to butterflies. 'Rustic Dwarfs' are my favourite because although the colours are variable, they are mostly in the brown shades which blend so well in garden schemes. Rudbeckias grow to between 18–24in (45–60cm) but they are sturdy and self-supporting and the flowers are produced from July until well into the autumn. Earlier flowers are possible with very

Fig 76 *Large-mesh clematis netting attached to stakes to support taller plants such as sweet peas.*

inappropriate, and many fences seem to be too low. Wires or strings are messy to arrange but they are not essential because support is easily provided with plastic netting which can be fixed on nails, about 2in (5cm) off the fence. The netting is not an eyesore, is soon covered by the plants, and is quickly dismantled.

Sweet peas can also be grown in beds, either on wigwams of bamboo canes or on semi-rigid clematis netting which is arranged as a circular column and secured by a few stakes. Otherwise, the dwarf varieties can be grown in beds with canes about 3ft (90cm) high at 6in (15cm) intervals and with string or netting tied to them. No sight delights more than a wall of sweet peas!

Sowing seed is often recommended as an autumn job and this will certainly result in earlier flowers than a spring sowing but I am not sure whether it is worth the trouble. I believe that sowing under glass in March or outdoors in April will be quite early enough but I have not mentioned the soil preparation which should be completed by late spring.

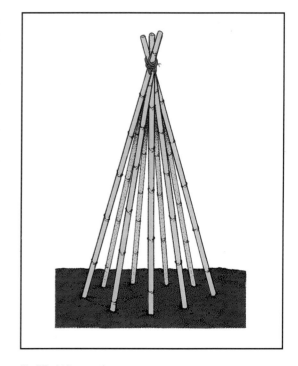

Fig 77 *Wigwam frame*

Fig 78(a)   Verbena being lifted from a container tray.
(b)   Verbena after having been extracted.

The perfectionist will excavate a trench about 1ft (30cm) deep and fill it with as much organic material as possible — horse manure, compost, rotted grass cuttings or peat — and then add a few ounces of bone meal. These measures are advisable for the best results because sweet peas like a good supply of nutrients and they dislike any tendency towards dryness at the roots. Watering, when necessary, and the regular removal of seed pods will prolong the display until late summer but if you insist on even later flowers, then I suggest that you sow a few seeds in late May. These should be placed in between the plants which are already growing and will ensure a fresh flush of bloom in August and onwards.

There are a number of different sweet pea groups such as 'Royals', 'Spencers' and 'Galaxies' and I suggest that you look through the Unwins catalogue to help your choice. Shorter types are also offered and I will mention a few such as 'Jet Set', 'Knee Hi' and 'Snoopea' which reach between 2–3ft (60–90cm) in height. The real midgets include 'Bijou', 'Little Sweetheart' and 'Cupid' — these can be grown without any support at all and make a most uncommon bedding display.

Verbena   HHA

Most verbena varieties are 8–10in (20–25cm) high with clusters of pretty flowers above dainty and neat foliage and their slightly spreading habit makes them ideal for edging the front of the border.

'Showtime' and 'Garden Party' are good mixtures of white, pink, red, purple and blue and 'Showtime Belle' and 'Sandy Scarlet', which were both Fleuroselect winners in 1988, are excellent examples of single colours. 'Tropic' won the same award about ten years ago but is still on offer and is a light red and of more upright habit than those other varieties.

Germination can be a problem with verbena and this is usually associated with a compost which is too wet at sowing time. It is advisable to avoid watering altogether if the compost is reasonably moist and just use a fine spray to settle the seed in place.

CHAPTER 12

Summer Plants: Old Favourites

The previous two categories of summer bedding plants are outstanding in many respects but appearance in the following list does not imply that the subjects are inferior in terms of beauty and appeal. Indeed, many are traditional flowers which have endeared themselves to gardeners for many decades and will continue to be grown, despite their limitations, by those who appreciate their qualities. The charm of nemesia, clarkia and godetia is evident to all who love plants but they have no staying power and unless you are prepared to replace them after a few weeks of delight, they should be used sparingly.

Abutilon   HHP
A half-hardy shrub which grows quickly and easily from seed and bears exotic flowers over a long period. Many varieties become quite large but 'Benary's Giant' is mis-named and will only reach about 20in (50cm)

Agrostemma (Corn Cockle)   HA
Disliked by farmers in its wild form, the corn cockle in cultivation bears lovely flowers but the spindly habit of growth makes it inappropriate for large groupings, although isolated specimens look well with more substantial subjects. 'Milas' is the only variety which is readily offered. It bears soft pink flowers and grows to about 2ft (60cm).

Althaea (Hollyhock)   HP,HA
The hollyhock has become a rarity in gardens but if a tall plant is required against a wall or fence, spectacular plants are achieved with the

Fig 79   Hollyhocks bring back memories of cottage gardens but it is not necessary to grow the very tall varieties in order to enjoy superb flowers.

'Summer Carnival' strain. The seed is better sown in January or February and the results will be 6ft (180cm) high plants with double flowers in a range of colours. A similar range is covered by the 'Majorette' strain but the maximum height will be 30in (75cm). Hollyhocks are perennial but older plants fall prey to rust disease and growing them as annuals, or biennials, is preferable.

Amaranthus (Love-Lies-Bleeding)   HHA
This is not everyone's choice as an elegant bedding plant but the hanging tassels do make an unusual feature. The catalogues also list varieties which have upright spikes such as 'Pygmy Torch'

in deep maroon and 'Green Thumb' with its long and long-lasting green spikes.

Anchusa   HA
For lovers of blue flowers, this is an intensely coloured and compact plant in the variety 'Blue Angel', 9in (22cm) and twice as tall with 'Blue Bird'. There is also a mixture called 'Dawn' which includes pink and white as well as shades of blue.

Arctotis (African Daisy)   HHA
Similar to dimorphotheca, these very showy daisies come in a wide range of pastel and bright colours, many with contrasting centres. The flowers close up in the evening but otherwise they are without vices and they make good cut blooms. Seed is usually sold as Large Flowered hybrids or as a mixture with the seed company's name. The normal height is 12–18in (30–45cm) and in a good summer, they are a glorious sight.

Brachycome (Swan River Daisy)   HHA
Lovely bushy plants with pleasantly scented flowers which are produced over a long period. Mixed seed produces flowers in many shades of blue as well as pinks and white but there is a single colour variety called 'Purple Splendour' which lives up to its name. The odd plant in a pot will be welcome for the fragrance which it gives to either home or greenhouse. The swan river daisy will grow to about 12in (30cm).

Calceolaria (Slipper Flower)   HHA
Better known as a greenhouse pot plant but there are some strains which make long-lasting summer bedders with characteristic yellow flowers. One is 'Sunshine' and the other, an F_1 hybrid bred by Floranova, is called 'Midas'. Both are 8–10in (20–25cm) and will thrive in sun or partial shade.

Calendula (Pot Marigold)   HA
Also known as the English marigold, the basic flower shape is recognisably that of the old-fashioned cottage plant which was often used as a herb but breeders have introduced con-

siderable variation in flower and habit. Of the smaller varieties, 'Fiesta Gitana' is a medal winner and the best known, but some of the shades of yellow and orange are undistinguished; selected colours from this variety are much more appealing. Taller types which are twice the height of 'Fiesta Gitana' include 'Art Shades', 'Kablouna' and 'Green Crown' which has a bright green centre. These varieties are typically 20–24in (50–60cm).

All of these marigolds flower profusely but pinching the shoots will encourage bushiness and dead-heading will prolong the show, although not beyond mid-summer.

Candytuft (Iberis)   HA
This is much admired as a perennial rockery plant but there are annual types which can make a useful contribution to summer bedding, either as a gap filler or in groups. White is the colour which we associate with candytuft but there are mixtures with reds, pinks as well as white and you may find a superior strain called 'Flash' in separate colours. All are 9–12in (22–30cm) high.

Fig 80 Candytufts make excellent border plants and are highly suitable for town gardens as they are tolerant of smoke and grime.

79

Chrysanthemum   HA

There are numerous types which can be used for summer bedding as well as those which start flowering in the early autumn. 'Tricolour' is a well-tried plant which has concentric bands of different colours running through the petals together with very graceful, fern-like foliage. 'Court Jesters' are also very colourful and 'Primrose Gem' is one of the prettiest flowers imaginable. All of these have a maximum height of 20–24in (50–60cm) with a lengthy flowering period from mid-July.

The later-flowering varieties make a splendid show from the early autumn when the summer display is growing tired and there are two varieties which are worthy of attention.

The first one is 'Fanfare', which has mostly double pompoms flowers on plants about 30in (70cm) high, whilst the second one, 'Autumn Glory', is a dwarf and mounding variety which is usually about 15in (40cm) in height. Both are F_1 hybrids and the displays will resist all but the most severe frosts and can be expected to flower until middle to late November. However, the quality of bloom is variable and the growth habits are not especially uniform. They are classed as hardy perennials but they may not survive very cold winters or wet soil and the stools should be lifted and stored if the plants are wanted for the following year.

Fig 81 Many of the early-flowering chrysanthemums will start their display in mid- to late August and continue for some weeks.

Clarkia   HA

The flowers look like small hollyhocks borne on wiry stems and the taller varieties such as 'Royal Bouquet', 24in (60cm), will benefit from some discreet support. 'Pulchella' is a much daintier plant, 12in (30cm), and there is an even shorter variety called 'Pink Ribbons'. 'Clarkia' is a most pleasing subject but it cannot be expected to give a long-lasting show.

Coreopsis (Tickseed)   HP

Fleuroselect awarded their first ever gold medal to a variety called 'Early Sunrise' and this caused some surprise because it cannot be described as an impressive plant. The flowers are yellow, semi-double and produced over the whole summer but there is no mass effect and the same descriptions can be applied to the other varieties, 'Cutting Gold' and 'Sunray'. All are rather neat-growing and reach about 18in (45cm); they are reliably perennial and flower easily in their first season.

Cosmos   HHA

Occasionally known as cosmea, it is a plant which is characterized by ferny foliage and single flowers with a central cone and in a good range of colours. The plants are tall, between 2–3ft (60–90cm) except for a few novelties like 'Sunny

Fig 82　Delphinium 'Blue Fountains', which will flower in the first season from an early sowing. Shown here in the Colegrave trial grounds.

Fig 83　The attractive foliage of cosmos adds variety to the display and the flowers always look agreeable, on the plant or in a vase.

Red' which is only 12in (30cm). The 'Sensation' mixture is commonly sold but new ones are introduced regularly such as 'Seashells' which has fluted petals, and a beautiful bi-colour called 'Daydream'.

Delphinium (Larkspur)　　　　　HP,HA

Catalogues use the word larkspur to describe the annual delphinium which are considerably shorter than the stately giants seen in the gardens of the devotees of these plants. The tallest delphiniums need staking but there are some perennials, which will flower in the first year from seed, but are only 3ft (90cm) high and are self-supporting except in very exposed positions.

'Blue Heaven' is sky blue with a white eye, 'Blue Fountains' is in many shades of blue and 'Magic Fountains' has pinks and purples in the colour range. Early spring sowing will ensure flowers in the first season and thereafter it is simple to get two flushes of bloom in the year by removing the faded flowers and stems. The foliage is most attractive in the border but beware, the young shoots are the favoured food of slugs which often eat them below soil level.

The annual varieties like 'Giant Imperial', 'Giant Double Hyacinth' and 'Tall Rocket' are between 2–3ft (60–90cm) high but there are taller ones such as 'Imperial Blue Bell' and 'Imperial White King'. Two dwarfs are well worth trying, 'Dwarf Hyacinth' in shades of pink, blue and white, and 'Tom Pouce' which is a most intense blue; both are 12in (30cm) high.

Dimorphotheca (Star of the Veldt)   HA

This plant is brilliantly effective for bedding but it much prefers well-drained soil and it must receive the maximum light. The flowers are similar to those of arctotis, daisy-like and often with a dark central disc. They come mostly in the orange and yellow part of the spectrum. Mixture varieties are often listed as 'New Hybrids' or 'Aurantiaca Hybrids' and there are some single colours like 'Dwarf Salmon' and the very eye-catching 'Glistening White' and 'Tetra Polestar'. The latter is the tallest at 15in (40cm) whilst the others are 9–12in (25–30cm) in height. You may find these plants listed as osteospermum in some catalogues.

Fig 84 Perhaps the best example of the beauty of godetia is the variety 'Salmon Princess'.

Eschscholzia (Californian Poppy)   HA

Unpronounceable it may be, but it really does come from California and obviously appreciates sunshine — it will therefore be a disaster in even partial shade. Some of the colours are very strong and do not easily blend with more formal bedding schemes but if they are grouped in the right position, these poppies will stop traffic! The blooms are short-lived but produced continuously and the display is helped by regular deadheading. 'Monarch Art Shades' and 'Ballerina' are good mixtures, 12in (30cm) high but there are some miniatures, 'Mission Bells' and 'Miniature Primrose' which are usually 6–9in (15–25cm) tall. There are a number of other single colour varieties — 'Orange King', 'Cherry Ripe' and 'Purple Violet' are examples which are 12–15in (30–40cm). Against the general advice for bedding subjects, these poppies are more productive in poor soil and their dislike of root disturbance means that they should be raised in containers or sown in situ.

Gaillardia (Blanket Flower)   HHA,HP

Another daisy-like flower which is more often considered as a perennial but frequently does not survive the winter in wet soils. There are, however, large and doubled-flowered varieties which are successful as annuals, although somewhat sprawling in their habit. The taller ones are 2–2½ft (60–75cm) and the dwarfs, such as 'Lollipop' and 'Goblin' are only 12in (30cm) — the latter bears some quite striking blooms with a red cone and central area and yellow outer fringes to the petals.

Godetia   HA

A highly regarded annual with trumpet-shaped flowers usually in shades of pink and orange, but with a relatively short flowering period. The taller varieties need supporting but even the shorter ones have an annoying tendency to fall over. 'Sybil Sherwood' and 'Salmon Princess' are amongst the most beautiful of flowers and the 'Azalea-Flowered Mixtures', all around 15in (40cm) tall, will not be disappointing.

Helichrysum (Straw Flower)   HHA

These have been grown for many years for use as dried flowers but the old varieties had rather insipid colours, making them uninteresting for bedding. Now there is 'Bright Bikini' which is only 12in (30cm) high and the mixture contains some good colours, the best of which is sold as 'Hot Bikini', a Fleuroselect bronze medal winner. There are some sold as separate colours but these are mostly very tall, 36–48in (90–120cm), of which 'Terracotta', 'Crimson Sky' and 'Orange One' are examples.

Heliotrope (Cherry Pie)   HHA

Surprisingly, this species has been ignored by plant breeders and there is only one variety,

Fig 85 There is only one variety of heliotrope available, called 'Marine', but it is delightful, with superb foliage and an unusual flower colour.

'Marine', in the principal catalogues although there is at least one mixture to be found which has mauve, lavender and purples. However, 'Marine' is superb with its lustrous deep purple flowers and really handsome foliage. The colour can be variable but this does not detract from the plant's value as a summer bedder of distinction. All the available heliotropes are 15–20in (35–50cm) and are wonderfully fragrant.

Lavatera (Mallow)   HA

This plant was virtually unknown until 'Silver Cup' became the first winner of a Fleuroselect silver medal and 'Mont Blanc' won a bronze award. 'Silver Cup' caught the imagination of gardeners with its gorgeous pink flowers with darker veins and, a few years later, 'Ruby Regis' made its debut with dark pink, almost red blooms.

Seed germinates readily and the seedlings are easily managed in cool conditions but it is important that they do not spend too much time in containers before planting out. if the roots become restricted, they often refuse to grow

Fig 86 The prize-winning lavatera 'Silver Cup' can be appreciated close up but the flower colouring also gives considerable impact towards the back of the display.

83

properly – and hot summers will shorten the flowering period if plants go dry.

Limonium (Statice)   HHA

Not a highly regarded flower for the garden but the modern strains should not be overlooked. They are, of course, grown commercially as desirable dried flowers but some new varieties make a considerable impact in summer bedding. The 'Fortress' strain is available in eight or nine separate colours on plants which grow about 20in (50cm) high and there are mixtures offered in most catalogues.

Matricaria (Feverfew)   HHA

More gardens should have these superb edging plants with their abundant chrysanthemum-type flowers which hide the foliage. 'White Gem', 'Golden Ball' and 'Tom Thumb White Stars' are all 8in (20cm), whilst 'Butterball' is slightly taller and 'Santana Lemon' is only 3–5in (8–12cm). As long as they are in a sunny position they perform well over quite a long period and are simply raised from seed.

Matthiola (Stocks)   HA,HHA,HB

One of the oldest flowers in cultivation, stocks have been cherished for hundreds of years

Fig 87   Statice, or sea lavender, is well known as a dried flower, but surprisingly its garden virtues are not often recognized.

Fig 88   The stocks are neglected by present day gardeners but they have enormous charm and a pleasant fragrance. Pictured at the Thomson and Morgan trial grounds near Ipswich.

because they are pretty and fragrant. The 'East Lothian' and 'Bromptons' are biennials although the former will respond to hardy annual treatment and the 'Ten Week' stocks, as the name suggests, are less than three months from sowing to flowering. The sweetest smelling are the 'Night Scented' stocks but their flowers are not very distinguished and they close by day.

Mesembryanthemum (Livingstone Daisy)   HHA

A memorable display in a memorable summer but when conditions are dull and miserable, these potentially dazzling daisies look distinctly dead. Not many varieties exist but there is the ever present mixture called 'Magic Carpet' which contains many bright and pastel colours and 'Lunette', sometimes known as 'Yellow Ice', which has bright yellow petals and a brown centre. They should be sown in late February or March because they are quite slow-growing; all varieties reach a maximum height of 4in (10cm).

Mimulus (Monkey Flower)   HHA

Plant breeders have changed the mimulus from an untidy marsh plant with indifferent colouring to a compact bedding subject bearing strongly coloured flowers and interesting markings. In the process, the characteristic scent has disappeared but the liking for moisture has persisted and so mimulus must not be allowed to go dry. Shady, moist positions are ideal and, being practically hardy, March-sown plants can be bedded out in late April and will begin flowering in May. The 'Malibu Hybrids' are in four separate colours and a mixture, and 'Calypso' is in most lists.

Nasturtium (Tropaeolum)   HA

Nasturtium is the subject of a love-hate relationship with many gardeners. It is admired for its hardiness and ease of cultivation but despised because it is often a home for caterpillars and sometimes the flowers are hidden by a vigorous canopy of foliage. In sunny places with free-draining soil, and without liberal feeding, the plants are dependable performers and the

Fig 89 *Nasturtium 'Alaska' is a most versatile blend of variegated foliage and colourful flowers which can be used in beds, baskets or tubs.*

Fig 90 *Nasturtium 'Alaska'.*

presence of caterpillars depends on fate and how much you want to prevent them. One variety, 'Alaska', has pretty variegated leaves but with only a moderate colour range. The 'Jewel' mixture, however, has good, bright hues and the flowers stand well above the foliage. 'Whirlybird' is a similar strain but some of the colours – cream, gold and scarlet – are available separately. 'Empress of India' is a good crimson and 'Peach Melba' has an interesting blend of red and yellow blooms. The seed is large and easily collected from the plants and as they are hardy, many plants will appear in the following year as self-sown seedlings.

Nemesia   HHA

A most beautiful and easily grown plant which flowers very quickly but is also finished quite soon. If the flower stems are cut down after the first flush, they will usually bloom again but nemesias will not give a sustained show. Most seed is sold mixed – 'Sparklers', 'Carnival', 'Tapestry' and 'Triumph' – but some have single colours like 'Blue Gem' and 'Blue Bird'. A red and white variety called 'Mello' was introduced with great gusto in 1989 but its garden performance was rather poor. The same variety appeared in two other catalogues, in the following year, under the names 'St George' and 'National Ensign' and it seems that the latter was the original name. 'Mello' was an old variety which had been 'rediscovered' and renamed and as far as can be detected, this happens quite often. (More frequently, batches of seed are bought by seed companies and then mixed according to their own formula; the resultant mixture is then given a name which is chosen by the company.

Nemophila (Baby Blue Eyes)   HA

Looking rather like blue buttercups, these pretty flowers enjoy cool and moist conditions and are useful for front row bedding. 'Insignis' has blue blooms with a white 'eye' and 'Five Spot', which is also called N. Maculata, has a lilac spot on each petal and light veining. 'Insignis' too, is sometimes sold under another name – N. menziesii. Both varieties mentioned are 6in (15cm) high.

Nigella (Love-in-a-Mist)   HA

Delicate foliage and ornamental seed heads are the bonus for growing nigella but the somewhat ragged flowers, in various pastel shades, do have an informal charm. 'Persian Jewels' is the common variety and the old cut flower, 'Miss Jekyll', which has clear blue and semi-double flowers, is still on offer. There is also a white version of 'Miss Jekyll' and recently, a smaller variety appeared which is called 'Dwarf Moody Blue'. The latter is 6–8in (15–20cm) whereas the others are 18in (45cm) tall.

Phacelia (Californian Bluebell)   HA

Intense blue, bell-shaped flowers are the hallmark of this subject and the dwarf species, P. campanularia, is excellent in sun or light shade, growing 9in (22cm) high. P. viscida is a similar blue but between 15–24in (40–60cm) and the flowers which have white centres are borne on spikes.

Poppy (Papaver)   HA,HB,HP

The 'Shirley' poppies are the best known with their single or double blooms and they are well represented in the seed catalogues in various mixtures. 'Mother of Pearl', also listed as 'Fairy Wings', is a blend of more subtle shades and at 10–14in (25–35cm) is almost 1ft (30cm) shorter than the usual 'Shirleys'. A strain called 'Reverend Wilkes' has a lovely range of colours and commemorates the man who developed these cultivated plants from the wild corn poppy.

Iceland poppies have the widest range of colours and are generally treated as hardy biennials – 'Oregon Rainbows' and 'San Remo' are examples and there is a very compact variety called 'Garden Gnome' which is 12in (30cm) tall. The opium poppies are usually listed as peony-flowered and the blooms are quite different to their relatives; some grow to about 3ft (90cm) and should be grown as hardy annuals.

The oriental poppy often bears blooms which are 8in (20cm) across and the vivid colours can overpower their bedding associates, especially as many plants are over 3ft (90cm) tall; 'Benary's Special Mixture' is an example. For less dominant plants there is a recently introduced F_1 hybrid called 'Summer Breeze' which is only 12–14in (30–35cm) and although a perennial, can be sown as a half-hardy annual.

Phlox   HHA
A popular bedding plant of yesteryear which now has difficulty in finding a place in the garden in competition with modern subjects. With adequate moisture, however, phlox will be in flower for a great deal of the summer. There are one or two taller varieties which are mostly perennial but the breeders' concentration has been on low plants such as 'Twinkles', 'Petticoat' and 'Dwarf Beauty' which are all between 6–8in (15–20cm) tall.

Salpiglossis (Painted Tongue)   HHA
Although the salpiglossis has a justifiably good reputation as a greenhouse plant, it has not yet become a reliable bedding plant. Breeders have been working on it but even the latest varieties are suspect in cool and wet summers and their slightly sprawling habit is not ideal for the garden. Nevertheless, the petunia-like flowers are stunning with strong colours and vivid veining or marbling of the petals. The seed is small but germinates freely and the plants can be grown in fairly cool conditions. 'Casino' and 'Ingrid' are varieties to try, as well as 'Splash' and 'Festival' which are all fairly compact – 12–18in (30–45cm).

Salvia (Sage)   HHA
A bed of scarlet salvia is an arresting sight and many gardeners are envious of the public displays in parks but I must say that the effect is too spiky for my taste. Unfortunately, there can be cultivation problems because the seed germination can be slow and erratic and the young plants need coddling in temperatures which must stay above 55°F (13°C), otherwise they begin to look sad. Even buying prime plants does not guarantee success because they too will deteriorate in low temperatures, especially if the hardening off process has been incomplete. Having said that, it is rewarding to succeed with

awkward subjects and, with the proper safeguards, a very colourful show will result.

One of the earliest introductions, 'Blaze of Fire', is still in the seed catalogues but neither its colour nor its performance compares with 'Volcano', 'Carabiniere', 'Fury', 'Vanguard' or 'Torpedo' and if you want other colours, the 'Pharaoh' mixture contains purples, lilacs and some bi-colours. There are also quite a few separate-coloured varieties in various blues and purples and another type of salvia, *S. Farinacea Victoria*, which has won an award for its elegant flowers and habit.

Scabiosa (Scabious,   HA
Pincushion Flower)
The annual scabious has never achieved the fame of its perennial relative but the flowers are of equal quality whose colour range includes blue, mauve, pink, white and even crimson. All the seed companies have mixtures of tall and short varieties and of special merit is one called 'Paper Moon' or 'Drumstick' which has pale blue flowers and seed heads which are in great demand for indoor decoration.

Schizanthus (Poor Man's   HHA
Orchid, Butterfly Flower)
This has long been an established pot subject for the cool greenhouse but very few people have tried it outside. It will do rather well in a sheltered and sunny spot where its small but brilliantly marked blooms can show to advantage. There are tall varieties, 3ft (90cm) high, but the dwarf types are more suitable for outdoors and even these will benefit from some discreet support – a few twigs will do. The plants must be pinched regularly to promote bushiness but otherwise they are without vices, although the flowering period will not be more than seven or eight weeks. The seed mixtures on offer are many and include 'Dwarf Bouquet', 'Hit Parade', 'Star Parade', 'Angel Wings' and 'Sweet Lips'.

Tagetes (Marigold)   HHA
Some seed catalogues use this heading to

distinguish the single-flowered marigolds from their double-flowered cousins but their other characteristics are identical. They are very simple to grow and will remain effective bedding plants for the whole summer. The 'Gem' series comes in tangerine, lemon and gold whilst 'Starfire' is a mixture of similar colours and a recent introduction, 'Paprika', has red flowers edged with a deep yellow. 'Florence' is a fairly recent award winner so too are 'Disco Orange' and 'Orange Jacket'.

Tithonia (Mexican Sunflower)   HHA

A glamorous, sun-loving flower which is reminiscent of the single dahlias, with slightly overlapping petals in rich orange and red hues. 'Goldfinger' is 30–36in (75–90cm) whilst 'Torch' and 'Yellow Torch' can reach 48in (120cm) but the blooms of these varieties are up to 3in (8cm) in diameter.

Zinnia (Youth and Old Age)   HHA

Just like the marigolds, these plants originate in Mexico but that is where the similarity ends because zinnias are unhappy without the sunshine of home. Given a fine summer and good soil, they are wonderful bedding subjects with many different kinds of flower – dahlia-flowered, scabious-flowered, cactus-flowered and so on. Thompson and Morgan's catalogue lists well over a dozen varieties because they sell widely in the US where zinnias are popular and highly successful. It is notable that Fleuroselect, the European organisation, has awarded five medals to

Fig 91   The aptly named Mexican Sunflower will certainly attract attention and is useful where taller subjects are required in the bedding scheme.

zinnias whereas the AAS winners exceed two dozens.

'Cherry' and 'Yellow Ruffles' won awards on both continents but they are not widely offered in Britain, although some of the shorter varieties such as 'Thumbelina', 'Peter Pan' and 'Persian Carpet' will perform creditably in reasonable summers and 'Pulchino' is well regarded in this respect.

The large seed germinates easily but the young plants will need cosseting for a while and hardening off carefully. The seedlings are better grown in containers because zinnias dislike root disturbance.

Fig 92(a) In cool, wet summers the zinnias are poor performers, but given good weather, they are glorious; especially the double-flowered varieties.

Fig 92(b) Lavatera 'Silver Cup', the first winner of a Fleuroselect silver medal, seen close up.

CHAPTER 13

Summer Plants: Uncommons and Unusuals

Gardeners are supposed to be somewhat conservative in their habits and do not readily accept innovations or the unknown but I am sure that this is true of most human beings and is not inherent in horticulture. That said, most people who grow plants do identify their favourites and tend to be loyal to them. Often, the reason for this is that we categorize plants into those which are easy to grow and give dependable results and those which are awkward and unreliable. This is fair enough except that sometimes plants get a bad name on the basis of one failure which might have been due to plain bad luck, or to some error in cultivation which could be easily rectified. With all natural processes, there are bound to be poor results or even no results at all but the accumulation of experience will enable you to minimize the possibilities of failure.

If I am flirting with a new subject for the garden (and I always am), I will persist if the attraction is great and hope that it will develop into a love affair. As with all love affairs, disappointment can be the outcome but I do believe that it is better to have loved and lost than never to have loved at all! By all means, plan your display on the basis of tried and tested performers but do also try something new each year because the joy of discovering a new gem for the garden is worth the chance of a little heartbreak.

Abelmoschus   HHA
A nice compact grower with very attractive foliage and hibiscus-like flowers which only last a day but are replaced throughout the season. The seed germinates readily but the seedlings need careful management and it is unlikely that the plants will perform well in a cool summer. 'Mischief' is the only variety sold and bears orange-red flowers with a white centre and prominent yellow stamens. It grows 10–12in (25–30cm) tall.

Achillea (Milfoil, Yarrow)   HP
Ferny foliage with flat flower-heads which show for most of the summer and make excellent cut flowers, fresh or dried. It reaches heights of 24in (60cm). Quite recently, the first F_1 hybrid was introduced – called 'Summer Pastels' which, although perennial, will flower in the first year if sown under glass in February or early March.

Adonis aestivalis (Pheasant's Eye)   HA
Deep red, cup-shaped flowers with very dark centres and very ornamental foliage. The Pheasant's Eye grows to 16in (40cm).

Alonsoa (Mask Flower)   HHA
Interesting flowers which are slightly reminiscent of small sweet peas. Alonsoa reaches heights of 15–18in (35–45cm). The species warscewiczii is a Peruvian plant with bright scarlet flowers but another species, *A. linearis*, can also be found. This is a tender perennial but responds well to half-hardy treatment and is constantly in flower.

Ammi (Bishop's Flower,   HA
Queen Anne's Lace)
This has large heads of white, lacy florets and

looks rather like an elegant cow parsley, sometimes given the varietal name 'Snowflake'. It grows to 36in (90cm).

Anagallis (Pimpernel, Poor Man's Weather Glass)   HA,HP

The Scarlet Pimpernel is occasionally seen growing in the fields but there is a cultivated blue form which was popular in Victorian gardens. It grows 6–12in (15–30cm) high.

Anoda   HHA,HHP

A tall – 48in (110cm) – free-flowering plant with large, single blooms in pink – the variety 'Opal Cup' – and there is a white one called 'Silver Cup'.

Argemone (Prickly Poppy)   HHA

Delicate papery flowers which show briefly but are regularly replaced. A. Grandiflora's flowers are white; A. mexicana's are in shades of yellow and there is also a variety called 'Yellow Lustre'. The prickly poppy reaches heights of 12–24in (30–60cm).

Asarina (Chickabiddy)   HHA,HHP

The species, A. procumbens, has pale yellow flowers on trailing foliage and it will thrive in shady positions. It reaches heights of 6–12in (15–30cm). There are also some climbing asarinas which are listed in Chapter 14, Summer Plants: Feature and Climbing Plants.

Asperula (Woodruff)   HA

Another shade-loving plant which produces clusters of mid-blue flowers which are very fragrant. It grows to 12in (30cm). The species is A. orientalis and is sometimes known as A. azurea.

Bartonia (Blazing Star)   HA

This is also known as mentzelia and is a beautiful, Californian flower, with deep yellow petals and prominent stamens, which closes without sunshine. The blooms are sweetly scented. The plant reaches heights of 18in (45cm).

Calandrinia (Red Maid, Rock Purslane)   HHA,HHP

The species C. meziesii is the red maid with perfumed, pink and red flowers whilst C. umbellata is called the rock purslane and needs dry, sunny weather to show off its crimson flowers. The plant grows to 12–18in (30–45cm).

Carthamus (Saffron Thistle)   HA

The Egyptians grew the species C. tinctorius to extract the yellow dye from the fluffy flowers. The plant grows to 30in (75cm). There is a cultivated form called 'Goldtuft'.

Celosia (Cockscomb)   HHA

Commonly used as a pot plant, these very brightly coloured subjects can be used for bedding. Be warned, however, the colours are such that the results may be startling. The plant reaches heights between 8–10in (20–25cm).

Centaurea (Cornflower)   HA

Once an old garden favourite, this is available in many different forms and colours. It grows to 24in (60cm) – the tallest varieties such as 'Blue Diadem' are for the back of the border – but there are dwarfs which only reach about 12in (30cm). 'Polka Dot' is available in mixed colours and 'Jubilee Gem', which is also known as 'Blue Boy', is a dark blue with double flowers. C. moschata, whose common name is sweet sultan, makes a lovely bushy plant which bears fragrant flowers made up of hundreds of narrow petals. The mixture, C. Imperialis, has a wide colour range and a recent introduction, 'The Bride', has outstanding white blooms.

Centaurium (Centaury)   HA

The species C. pulchellum is a dainty plant with loose clusters of dark pink blooms which will succeed in most places but prefers moist conditions. The plant grows to 6in (15cm).

Clary (Salvia horminium)   HA

This is grown for its colourful bracts, which – unlike flowers – are really modified leaves, but the floral effect is bright and unusual. Mixtures are available but separate colours are also sold in the 'Claryssa' series – blue, pink or white. Clary reaches heights of 18in (45cm).

Cleome (Spider Flower)   HHA

Very graceful blooms which will attract the attention of neighbours and bees and are commonly sold as mixtures which include pinks, purple and white although separate-coloured varieties can be found such as 'Cherry Queen', 'Pink Queen', 'Violet Queen' and a white one called 'Helen Campbell'. The plant grows to 36in (90cm).

Collinsia (Chinese Houses)   HHA

A Californian flower with two lips, the upper white and the lower a light purple. The plants are not at all difficult and will do well in light shade. They grow to 12–18in (30–45cm).

Convolvulus (Dwarf Morning Glory)   HA

These relatives of the dreaded greater bindweed are extremely pretty annuals which have very brightly coloured flowers, often with contrasting centres, but the plants are nothing like the climbers and are very neat and compact. Colours range from purple and blue to pink and white. There are some separate colours such as 'Royal Ensign', which is deep blue with a white and yellow centre, and 'Blue Ensign', which is a different shade of blue but otherwise similar. It grows to 6–12in (15–30cm).

Cotula (Pincushion Plant)   HHA

Small, spherical flowers on a plant which is very useful for creeping over stones and the edges of paths. It grows to 3–6in (7–15cm) – there is a tall variety called 'Turbinata' which has similar blooms but grows to about 24in (60cm)

Craspedia   HHA

Globular flowers make a nice change and these yellow ones have the added advantage of drying well for indoor decoration. They reach heights of 9–18in (22–45cm). A taller variety, 'Goldstick', grows to about 24in (60cm).

Crepis (Hawksbeard)   HA

Few catalogues list this plant but it is well worth looking for. The species *C. rubra*, with its pale pink flowers, is most usually sold but there is a white form called 'Snowplume' with a light yellow centre. The plants will not normally flower until late July but, thereafter, the show is quite persistent. Hawksbeard reaches heights of 12in (30cm).

Cuphea (Mexican Cigar Plant)   HHA

Another greenhouse plant which can succeed in sheltered areas of the garden. Its tubular flowers are available in various shades of red with purple and white tips. The species *C. ignea* and another variety called 'Firefly' are readily available and there is a newer and taller novelty, *C. viscosissima*. The plant grows to 12–18in (30–45cm).

Echium (Viper's Bugloss)   HA

E. vulgare bears numerous spikes of blue flowers which are roughly cup-shaped and much appreciated by bees. There is a hybrid mixture listed in a couple of catalogues which are in shades of pink, blue and purple and these plants will make a lovely erect display. The plant grows to 12in (30cm).

Emilia (Tassel Flower)   HHA

A tropical but easily raised plant which has grey-green foliage and bears a large number of red, orange or deep yellow tassels. It reaches heights of 18–24in (45–60cm).

Erigeron (Fleabane)   HHA, HP

This plant reaches heights of 6–18in (15–45cm). 'Profusion' is the best-known variety and bears masses of daisy-shaped flowers which change from white to dark pink as they mature. 'Azure Jewel', 'Azure Beauty' and 'Pink Jewel' have similar flowers but only grow to 24in (60cm).

Eustoma (Prairy Gentian)   HHA

The original *E. grandiflorum* from North America

has lovely deep blue flowers for most of the summer but there are now some F_1 hybrids available in mixed colours and a series called 'Yodel' which has blue, pink and white flowers — available separately or as a formula mixture. The eustomas dislike root disturbance and should be pricked out into containers whilst very small; they are also slow-growing in the first few weeks. They grow to 15–18in (38–45cm).

Gilia (Birds' Eyes, Queen Anne's Thimbles)   HA
Charming globular flowers in dense clusters above fern-like, compact foliage. This plant reaches heights of 12–15in (30–38cm).

Gomphrena (Globe Amaranth)
This plant reaches heights of 12in (30cm). Its everlasting flowers resemble small, coloured pine cones in red, pink or purple but a fairly recent variety called 'Buddy', which is only half the normal height, has impressed many people with its bedding qualities. The species, *G. haageana*, is something of a colour rarity with its orange flowers.

Gypsophila (Baby's Breath)   HA
Flower arrangers love the wispiness of this plant, especially with the traditional white flowers, but sometimes it can be rather disappointing in the garden. There are pink and red varieties and if these are used with more solid subjects, they can give a delightful effect of 'see through' haze. The plant grows to 18in (45cm).

Helianthus (Sunflower)   HA
An arresting flower which is normally grown as a single specimen in order to attract local newspaper photographers or to delight young children. In France, however, it is grown *en masse* presumably to start a cooking oil lake! However, for those who do not own a ten-hectare field, there is the variety 'Teddy Bear' which bears large – 6in (15cm) – double blooms on plants which only grow to 24in (60cm).

Hibiscus   HHA,HHP
This is more widely known as an exotic house-plant or as a tender shrub, but there are a number of varieties which can be treated as half-hardy annuals and will flower in the same year if sown very early. They are not hardy plants but some will live through mild winters and will consequently flower earlier and more profusely in subsequent seasons. They grow to 18–48in (45–120cm). The 'Disco' series is at the low end of the height range and the F_1 hybrid 'Dixie Belle' is slightly taller. Another F_1, 'Southern Belle', will reach 4ft (120cm) if conditions are favourable. 'Cream Cup' and 'Sunnyday' are also worthy of mention but all the varieties named have large and exquisite flowers.

Impatiens balsamina (Balsam)   HHA
The name balsam covers the native European noli-tangere, touch-me-not, as well as the species which was imported from the Himalayas and has become an invasive weed along river banks. Their height ranges between 9–22in (22–30cm). The cultivated varieties are easily grown and do add something different to the summer display; the flowers are borne close to the stems and provide an unusual blend of foliage and colour. Some varieties, like the 'Camellia Flowered', reach about 19in (45cm) whilst 'Tom Thumb' is half that height; both have double flowers in pinks, white or red. There are also some novelty bi-colours — 'Strawberry Ice' and 'Peppermint Stick'.

Layia (Tidy Tips)   HA
Cheerful flowers which have yellow petals, each tipped with white. The plant grows to 15in (40cm).

Leptosiphon (Star Dust)   HA
Masses of tiny, star-shaped flowers in a wide range of colours but the early summer display is rather short-lived. The plant reaches heights of 4–6in (10–15cm).

Limnanthes (Poached Egg Plant)   HA
Of all the plants in my garden, I think that this

93

Fig 93 *Balsam adds a touch of variety because of the shape of the plant and its habit of producing flowers in the leaf axils, like this 'Camellia Flowered' example.*

Fig 94 *As well as being one of the easiest plants to grow, Limnanthes is one of the most appealing even though the flowering period is fairly restricted.*

one attracts most attention. The combination of white and bright yellow flowers gives a gorgeous carpet effect which lasts for some weeks and self-sown seedlings will often flower later in the year. These seedlings are readily transplanted elsewhere in the garden or the plants can easily be confined to one place and are not at all invasive. Bees and hover-flies seem to find limnanthes more desirable than any other flower. The plant grows to 6in (15cm).

Linaria (Toadflax)   HA
Most of the linaria species are perennial but there are a few annuals for summer flowering such as 'Fairy Bouquet' and 'Fairy Lights' which resemble miniature snapdragons, in quite a wide colour range. Linaria grows to 9in (22cm).

Linum (Flax)   HA
The common flax is found in many catalogues and not only is it the source of linseed oil, but the sky blue flowers are really brilliant. This plant is 2–3ft (60–90cm) high and the more popular varieties like *L. grandiflorum rubrum* – which has rich scarlet blooms – and 'Bright Eyes' – which is white with a red eye – are never more than 18in (45cm) tall.

Lonas   HA
This is one of the more neglected everlasting flowers which bears clusters of deep yellow blooms – on bushy plants reaching 15–18in (35–45cm) – which last for many weeks. Lonas is in flower for most of the summer.

Lupinus (Lupin)   HA
What, you might ask, is such a familiar plant doing under the heading of 'Uncommons and Unusuals'? Well, the perennials are commonplace but few gardens seem to house any of the annual varieties such as 'Pixie Delight' or 'Lulu' which are only 12in (30cm) high. So too is the species *L. texensis* which has blue and white flowers but there is an attractive yellow species from Europe called *L. luteus* which reaches 24in (60cm).

Malope   HA 36in (90cm)

One of the cottage garden flowers of yesteryear which really deserves a revival. The blooms are large and delightful and betray the malope's connection with the mallow family. The mixed varieties bear pink, red and white flowers whilst the species *trifida grandiflora* bears deep purple blooms and a variety called 'Vulcan' bears flowers of the deepest red.

Nolana   HHA

A newcomer to the bedding scene. The plants have a low and creeping habit with very pretty, trumpet-shaped flowers which are slightly similar to gloxinia. Blue is the dominant colour but the flowers have a white throat and yellow centre and the variety 'Blue Bird' is listed in quite a number of the popular seed catalogues. Nolana is also being grown by the bedding trade and it is likely that plants will be increasingly available. Nolana grows to 6–9in (15–22cm).

Oenothera (Evening Primrose)   HHA

There are a few species which can be grown as annuals – including *O. acaulis*, *O. missourensis* and *O. odorata*. The first-named bears large flowers which open white and turn deep pink; the others are smaller and the main characteristics are fragrance and blooms which open in the evening. Oenothera reaches heights of 6–12in (15–30cm).

Osteospermum   HHA

This is a thoroughly confusing heading which should include Tripteris and Dimorphotheca – the latter is listed in the last chapter – but in the seed catalogues, different varieties are shown under at least two of the three generic titles. However, whichever name they answer to, they are vividly coloured flowers and the mixtures' colour range embraces red, pink, orange and white, mostly with contrasting centres. Worthy of special note are 'Dwarf Salmon' at 9in (22cm) and 'Gaiety' which has bright orange petals with a black centre and grows up to 24in (60cm) tall. The bad news is that the flowers need sunshine

in order to open and 'Gaiety' is the worst in this respect.

Polygonum   HHP

One species, *P. capitatum*, is a tender perennial but grows and flowers quickly enough to be used as an annual. The plant grows up to 6in (15cm) tall and needs well-drained soil. Its reddish foliage and small pink flowers look pretty for many weeks.

Reseda (Mignonette)   HA

Many gardeners are not impressed with these flowers but everyone agrees that the scent is delicious. The basic flower colour is green and this is true of 'Fragrant Beauty' although 'Red Monarch' and 'Machet' are strongly tinged with red. The plant reaches heights of 12in (30cm).

Sanvitalia (Creeping Zinnia)   HA

A little-known but easily grown ground cover plant. The species, *S. procumbens*, bears yellow flowers with a purple centre although there is a double-flowered form which bears golden flowers. The variety 'Gold Braid' is also double-flowered with deep yellow petals and 'Mandarin Orange' won an All American Selection (AAS) award. Sanvitalia grows to 6in (15cm).

Silene (Catchfly)   HP

Silvery tufts of foliage, which in the case of the species *S. schafta* bears sprays of pink flowers. The variety 'Robin White Breast', on the other hand, bears white flowers which are double and balloon-shaped. Although perennials, these plants will flower in the first season and over quite a long period. The plant reaches heights of 6in (15cm).

Thymophylla (Dahlberg Daisy)   HHA

A pleasantly fragrant subject with some finely divided foliage, a mounding and spreading habit and a long show of yellow flowers. This plant is not listed in many seed catalogues but is receiving attention from some of the world's largest breeders and you may find that it becomes a high-profile bedding subject in the future. It grows to 6in (15cm).

Ursinia HHA

Yet another of the South African daisies but one which has aromatic foliage and flowers which do tend to stay open, even in slightly dull weather. There are not many varieties on offer but most seed companies have hybrid mixtures. Ursinia grows to 18in (45cm).

Venidium (Monarch of the Veldt) HHA

The common name will leave you in no doubt as to the origins of this plant but its flowers are semi-double and look more like sunflowers than daisies. The plant grows to 24in (60cm); the blooms are 4in (10cm) across with a contrasting base to the petals and a dark central disc. They are very striking and enhance any display. A recent variety, 'Zulu Prince', sports cream petals which make the contrasting zones even more eye-catching.

Fig 95   Venidium 'Orange Surprise' is a lesser-known flower and is excellent for borders and summer bedding.

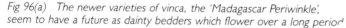

Fig 96(a)   The newer varieties of vinca, the 'Madagascar Periwinkle', seem to have a future as dainty bedders which flower over a long period

Fig 96(b)   A close-up of the magnificent Venidium 'Orange Surprise'.

Vinca (Madagascar Periwinkle)   HHA

Sometimes listed under the name catharanthus, it is normally grown as a greenhouse subject but will succeed in a warm position in the garden, reaching heights of 6–9in (15–22cm). Mixtures are available with pink, white or combinations of these colours but you should watch out for two new series – the 'Coolers' and 'Sahara Madness' – and a variety called 'Polka Dot' was an AAS winner. All the vincas flower endlessly!

Viscaria   HA

A long-flowering and neat subject whose flowers usually have a dark eye. It comes in a good colour range – seed companies offer mixtures but you may encounter the magenta, 'Maggie May', or 'Blue Angel' and 'Rose Angel', both of which

have been honoured in RHS trials. Viscaria grows to 9–15in (22–35cm).

Xeranthemum (Common Immortelle) HA

The wild plant grows in the Near East and Southern Europe and is noted for its whitish, woolly leaves and everlasting flowers. The seed mixtures contain pinks, lilacs, purples and white but perhaps the most distinctive colour is in a variety called 'Purple Violet'. Xeranthemum grows to 24in (60cm).

With very few exceptions, the 'Uncommons and Unusuals' will have to be grown from seed because they are not available as plants and I should add that I have only included a small selection; there are hundreds more waiting to be discovered by the adventurous gardener.

CHAPTER 14

Summer Plants: Feature and Climbing Plants

Most displays are improved by planting foliage subjects in order to balance high-impact colours or to allow a pleasant transition between contrasting areas. The foliage, whatever colour it may be, becomes a highlight in a sea of flowers but these feature plants can also be used in groups or as alternate plantings with flowering subjects. Many of the popular bedding plants are quite short in stature and the addition of something taller, sporting different features, will add to the interest and variety of the show. As well as the foliage plants, there are some flowers which are ideal for this purpose but I do believe that an increased emphasis on foliar displays is long overdue.

Abutilon   HHS
Most of these tender shrubs are very handsome subjects for the garden and have the bonus of bearing exotic-looking flowers – but it is the shape and texture of the leaves which suit the bedding purpose so well.

The variety A. striatum Thompsonii has lovely variegated leaves but it must be grown from cuttings and given greenhouse protection for the winter. Most of the seed merchants offer at least one variety and the plants are easily raised if warm conditions can be provided from spring onwards. The shrubs grow 24–60in (60–150cm) high.

Amaranthus (Love Lies Bleeding)   HHA
Some of the flowering types have very decorative foliage but some varieties particularly accentuate this feature – 'Illuminations', 'Flamingo Fountains' and 'Joseph's Coat' are such. (The last-named will make you blink and I think it needs courage to plant it.) Amaranthus grows to 24–36in (60–90cm).

Atriplex (Red Orache)   HHA
The variety, P. purpurea, grows quickly and the dark purple leaves look particularly well in a border with red or blue flowers. In a good summer, it will reach over 5ft (150cm) – the average height lies between 36–60in (90–150cm) – but it is easily restrained and if the growing tips are removed, it will make quite a bushy specimen.

Brassica (Ornamental Cabbage)   HA
Unbelievably coloured examples of the mundane vegetable which certainly attract attention – perhaps too much for some tastes. There is also a lettuce called 'Red Salad Bowl' and a technicolour kale which was selected as a Fleuroselect novelty and which is called 'Red and White Peacock'. The leaf colouration of these plants is activated when lower temperatures prevail and they are at their most vivid during the winter – perhaps fortunately. They grow to 12in (30cm).

Bupleurum (Sickle Hare's Ear)   HP

The unusually shaped leaves and clusters of lime green, yellow flowers will attract floral arrangers from miles around. The plant looks charming in sun or light shade. The species B. falcatum and a variety called 'Green Gold' are available. It grows 18–60in (45–150cm) tall.

Canna (Indian Shot)   HHP

This is frequently used in park displays, especially the bronze-leaved type, to add an exotic and elevating look to the border. Flowers in shades of yellow, red and pink will appear in the first season if the seed is sown early but canna roots must be protected from frost and should be stored in the same way as dahlia tubers. Canna grows to 36in (90cm).

Celosia (Cockscomb, Prince of Wales Feathers)   HHA

The crested blooms of the cockscombs are not often used in the garden but the Prince of Wales Feathers bear some really elegant plumes, which, if planted in moderation, look highly effective. The Japanese-bred 'Castle' series is tall with absolutely stunning colours – reds, pinks and yellows – whilst the Ballet strain and the award-winning 'Dwarf Fairy Fountains' are equally colourful but only 12–15in (30–38cm) – Celosia grows to 12–30in (30–75cm).

Centaurea   HHP

Quite different to its cornflower relatives, the C. candidissima species is grown for its silvery foliage and the leaves are larger than those of Cineraria Maritima. The plant grows 12–15in (30–35cm) high.

Cerastium (Snow in Summer)   HP

A plant which grows to 8in (20cm). it is principally grown for its white flowers in late spring but the almost white, woolly foliage is a useful foil throughout the year. Beware; it will spread quite quickly.

Cineraria maritima   HHP

The most popular of the silver leaf bedding plants which is sometimes listed as Senecio cineraria and makes a lovely combination with every colour imaginable. 'Silver Dust' is the most common and the shortest variety at 8in (20cm) – but there is also 'Cirrus' which is about twice that height. These plants will often survive a mild winter and will grow much larger, but they are easily cut back.

Coleus (Flame Nettle)   HHP

A much appreciated pot plant which can offer brightly coloured leaves in the garden as long as

Fig 97 The rich colours of coleus, the flame nettle, are equally eye-catching whether outdoors or under glass.

the weather is reasonably kind. Two strains which gained an RHS award of merit are 'Carefree' and 'Wizard' but there are some varieties which can be grown from seed and produce plants whose markings are identical one to the other. This means that you can more easily design a colour scheme. (Some examples are 'Volcano', 'Pagoda' and 'Highland Fling'. The plant grows 12–18in (30–45cm) tall.

Cordyline   HHP
This is another plant which is favoured by public parks to add elegant height to a bedding scheme. The usual choices are C. australis and C. indivisa, both of which have sword-shaped leaves – the latter with red and yellow splashes on the foliage. neither is likely to survive anything but the mildest winter. Cordyline reaches heights of 24–36in (60–90cm).

Eryngium (Sea Holly)   HP
Not everyone loves the spiny appearance of this plant, E. maritinum, but the glaucous foliage and pale blue flowers are quite intriguing. Other species such as E. alpinum, E. giganteum and E. bourgatii possess equally striking looks but they are all perennial and flowers will not normally appear in the first season from seed. The plant grows to 18–24in (45–60cm).

Eucalyptus (Gum Tree)   HHP
The usual species for foliar effect is E. globulus, the blue gum, and the juvenile silver-blue leaves are lovely but there are many more in this family of trees which make beautiful features in the flower beds. Although all the eucalyptus come from Australia, some of the species are remarkably hardy and you may find that if your infant tree is left in the garden, it becomes a giant in a surprisingly short time – 20–60ft (6–18m).

Euphorbia (Spurge)   HHA,HP
This is a most rewarding genus for gardeners who want something out of the ordinary, and it contains a diverse range of plants. E. marginata has grey, green leaves edged with white and is grown

as an annual; E. heterophylla is another splendid annual which is best described as a border poinsettia and E. wallichii has dark green leaves with a white central rib and yellow bracts in early summer. The plant's height reaches 18–36in (45–90cm).

Fuchsia   HHP
Many gardens house specimens of hardy fuchsias which provide a summer-long show, whilst others house the tender varieties which are only temporary residents. With their pendulous habit, much of the beauty of the flowers is not evident when viewed from above but as dot plants or groups, they are most agreeable. More spectacular, but much more trouble, is to grow standards with stems of 2ft (60cm) or more when they provide an umbrella of blooms. It requires at least one season to grow a stem of sufficient length and these specimens will need staking and, of course, a frost-free home for the winter. Having gone to all this trouble, these standards can be used for many years and look magnificent.

The foliage of fuchsias is on the whole very

Fig 98 Many varieties of fuchsia, especially the smaller-flowered ones, are perfectly resilient in the open garden. This diminutive example is 'Son of Thumb'.

ordinary, but there is an exception with *F. magellanica* whose leaves are exceptionally coloured in pink, purple and cream. The species grows into a large bush but there is a form called 'Versicolour' which grows to about 18in (45cm) and makes an excellent subject for moist and shady situations. As far as I am aware, the shorter form is not grown from seed.

Glaucium (Horned Poppy)   HB

Deeply cut, silvery-white foliage is the hallmark of *G. flavum*, with the bonus of large poppy-like flowers in deep yellow. When the flowers die, the plant produces huge, ornamental seed pods. Glaucium stands at 12–18in (30–45cm).

Helichrysum petiolatum   HHP

Unlike the everlasting flowers which bear the same generic name, this is a wonderful foliage plant which is now being used extensively in containers and hanging baskets. The leaves, which are covered in a delicate white down, are sufficiently robust to withstand garden conditions and if the extending stems are pinched out, the plants become bushy and quite dense. Three or four different forms are sold; 'Limelight' – a lovely lime green colour – and Variegata – grey with cream variegations – are the most common ones. Seed is not available for these plants which must be purchased as pot-grown or as rooted cuttings and they require over-wintering in a greenhouse. This plant reaches 18in (45cm) in height.

Herbs

Naturally, herbs may be grown for reasons other than cosmetic ones, but some of them are exceedingly useful for ornamental situations:

Angelica archangelica   HB

With the most heavenly name in horticulture, angelica makes a splendid feature against a wall or fence. Like most herbs, it requires a sunny position and will flower dramatically in its second season and then die.

Borago officinalis (Borage)   HA

Whilst the foliage is not outstanding, it is a pleasant colour and texture and the blue flowers are very pretty. The plant grows to 24in (60cm).

Foeniculum vulgare (Fennel)   HP

Fennel is also a tall plant which has graceful, feathery foliage. The foliage is usually green but there is a bronze form. Fennel reaches 48in (120cm) in height.

Melissa officinalis (Lemon Balm)   HP

This makes a bushy plant which never looks out of place and you may be able to find the golden and variegated forms which are handsome. It reaches 24in (60cm).

Ocimum basilicum (Basil)   HA

'Dark Opal' is a variety of sweet basil with purple leaves which enhances the garden as well as the salad bowl. 'Purple Ruffles' is a similar plant which won an AAS award some years ago. The plant's height ranges between 18–24in (45–60cm).

Origanum onites (Pot marjoram)   HP

Marjoram looks very much at home in flower beds and its own pinky, purple blooms are not without charm. There is a golden-leaved form which does quite well in the shade. Marjoram grows to 12in (30cm).

Petroselinum (Parsley)   HB,HA

This highly decorative herb makes a marvellous space-filler amongst flowering plants and is very suitable as background foliage for shorter subjects, or as a ground base for tall flowers. There are many varieties offered with different heights and colouring but typically the foliage is dense, mid-green, and attractively curled. Germinating the seed is sometimes awkward but a fairly dry compost will improve results. Parsley grows to heights ranging between 12–24in (30–60cm).

Salvia officinalis (Sage)   HP

There are numerous herb sages with delightful

foliar colour – Purpurescens with purple leaves; Tricolour with green, white and pink leaves and Icterina with yellow variegations. All are easily propagated from cuttings taken in the summer or early autumn. The plant reaches 18–30in (45–70cm).

Grasses

Ornamental grasses offer a superb contrast to conventional bedding plants because of their graceful, narrow leaf shapes and pretty seed heads. *Agrostis* bears tiny, spiked heads; *Briza*, the quaking grass, bears pendulous flower pods; *Lagurus* (Hare's tail) bears lovely soft heads; *Hordeum* bears silvery-grey plumes and *Pennisetum* is graced by white or purple 'feathers'. Thompson and Morgan list about a dozen species of grass which are hardy or half-hardy annuals, as well as others which are hardy perennials.

Hypoestes (Polka Dot Plant)   HHA
A popular house-plant which may, one day, become as common as *Cineraria maritima* for foliar bedding – it will perform well as a garden subject in any position which is neither hot nor dry. The plants are naturally self-branching but it is advisable to pinch out some of the growing tips to ensure bushy growth. Cuttings root easily but it is simpler to sow seed in the spring, making sure that the plants are hardened off before setting them out. 'Pink Splash' is a variety to look out for. The Polka Dot plant reaches 8–10in (20–25cm).

Kochia (Burning Bush)   HHA
Looking rather like small conifers, kochia make very interesting dot plants but if you want a really unusual feature, plant them about 1ft (30cm) apart and you will have a lovely, temporary hedge. This will make a fine backcloth for low-growing flowers because although the main appeal is the late summer and autumnal shades of brown and red, the juvenile foliage is a beautiful soft green. The only readily available variety is *K.*

trichophylla – one variety called K. 'Acapulco Silver' won an AAS award, but is not widely listed. Kochia grows to 24–36in (60–90cm).

Lantana (Shrub Verbena)   HHP
These shrubs are commonly grown in Mediterranean countries, displaying verbena-like flower-heads which change colour from yellow to lilac as they mature. Seed can be bought which also produces white and yellow flowers but germination is erratic and can take a couple of months. The

Fig 99   Lantana should be treated as a tender bedding plant.

102

plants develop into small shrubs and their shape is improved by pinching out the growing tips of early shoots – once the flowering commences, it continues throughout the summer and autumn. Mature plants can be cut down and potted for greenhouse storage and, when growth restarts, cuttings can be rooted for the following season. Lanatas reach 18–30in (45–75cm).

Molucella (Bells of Ireland)   HHA
Grown for its green, bell-shaped calyces, these plants provide a welcome and tasteful relief from intensely coloured bedding plants. Their fragrance is pleasant and the flower stems are greatly appreciated by flowers arrangers, who can use the plant either in its freshly cut or dried form for winter decoration. Bells of Ireland reach heights of 36in (90cm).

Plectranthus coloides marginatus   HHP
(Variegated Swedish Ivy)
It's a terrifying botanical name but the plant has come to the fore only in recent years and has proved its value as a foliage subject for tubs and baskets. If the tips of shoots are pinched out, plectranthus makes a bushy backdrop for flowers of any colour and in its own right, the bright green leaves edged in creamy-white give a cheerful effect. As far as I am aware, the plant is not grown from seed and therefore you will have to buy it potted or as cuttings. It is not especially tender but will need protection from sub-zero temperatures. Plectranthus reaches heights of 15in (37cm).

Pyrethrum   HP,HHA
The genus is noted for its daisy-like flowers, but there are a couple of species which are invaluable for their leaf shape and colour. *P. aureum*, which is sometimes listed as Parthenium, makes a 4in (10cm) carpet of delicate light green-yellowish foliage. It does also flower but these are indeed daisy-like – although inconspicuous – and they do not usually arrive until after mid-summer. The variety 'Golden Moss' is widely available.

Ricinus (Castor Oil Plant)   HHA
This plant grows 36–72in (90–180cm) high. This bronze-leaved version of the well-known houseplant is much loved by parks and display gardens and it is only in such situations that the larger varieties will fit. They are, however, truly impressive subjects and, especially when they are young and small, can be used with great effect in garden bedding schemes. 'Impala' is a smaller variety which has an almost dark red colouring but will reach 4ft (120cm) in a favourable position and season. 'Carmencita' is the parks' choice and is half as tall again.

Swiss Chard   HA,HB
At one time, quite a number of beetroot varieties were grown for their remarkable foliar effect but nowadays only the spinach beets are used – and then only by the brave! Rhubarb chard, often called Ruby, has scarlet stems and leaf ribs and a seed mixture called 'Swiss Rainbow' produces plants with white or red stems and vivid green leaves. The plant reaches 12–15in (30–38cm).

Zea (Sweet Corn)   HHA
The variety *Z. japonica* has green leaves with narrow, white stripes and cobs with red, gold or orange seeds. 'Quadricolour' has a red tinge to the green and white foliage and it does not produce cobs. Another variety, 'Strawberry Corn', has oval cobs which are maroon or dark red. Like some of the other feature plants, zeas can look rather startling in the wrong setting and they all grow to about 4ft (120cm).

All the foliage feature plants listed in this section, even though they may be perennials, will grow sufficiently in the first season from seed to make a contribution to bedding schemes. Another alternative is to use hardy perennials as a permanent framework for annual flowers and feature plants, and the following are excellent foliage subjects which will flower in the second season from seed.

103

Anaphalis margaritacea — everlasting white blooms and grey foliage — I5in (37cm).
Lobelia cardinalis — red flowers and bronzy red leaves — 24–30in (60–75cm).
Santolina chamaecyparissus — silver, woolly leaves, yellow flowers with purple centres — 24in (60cm).
Stachys lanata — silver, hairy foliage and fluffy purple flowers — 24in (60cm).

Climbers

Of all the various categories of plants mentioned in this book, I suspect that this one is the least employed for garden decoration, and yet everyone has vertical structures which would benefit from cosmetic treatment. I know that some gardeners are reluctant to plant conventional climbers against the house wall for fear of damage to the building or simply because most of the subjects used are permanent by nature and might be difficult to remove. The plants listed here – with a few exceptions – are half-hardy and although some of them are quite vigorous, they will not survive the winter. Hence, you can grow a couple of them each year and yet be confident that they will not exploit your hospitality.

Fences, sheds, garages as well as the house walls can be made receptive to these climbers just by the provision of some unobtrusive support at strategic places; but there are other situations which may not be quite so obvious. Some of the shrubs and trees in the garden will make excellent hosts for those climbers which are not too rampant and I will give one example. We all love forsythia and revel in its radiance in the spring but after the post-flowering pruning and for the rest of the year, it presents a very ordinary sight – it is in fact decoratively redundant until the next year. Forsythia, however, makes an ideal prop for a summer climber.

The same principle can be applied to many other plants, even those which may flower during the summer. Clematis tends to flower for four or five weeks and, at other times, it could be the ideal vehicle for a climbing annual. Pyracantha is even better for carrying a flowering passenger in the summer months. The visitor will have disappeared before the firethorn berries dazzle in the autumn. The sunny side of hedges can also be used for the same purpose and there are many other ways in which to use climbers – all you have to do is to apply some vertical thinking.

Asarina (Chickabiddy) HHA

This name appeared in the chapter 'Uncommons and Unusuals' when one species was recommended as a spreading, ground cover plant but most of this genus comprises climbers. A sunny position is needed for good flowering performance and the plants will need tying to supports – the beautiful blooms are ample reward for the effort. The variety *A. scandens* bears dark blue flowers; *A. erubescens'* flowers are dark pink and *A. barclaiana's* are pink or purple.

Campsis (Trumpet Vine) HHA

A rapid grower which is self-clinging and bears brilliant orange and red flowers in clusters. A sunny spot is preferred and the plant is quite vigorous; there is also the possibility that it could survive a mild winter in some areas.

Cardiospermum (Balloon Vine, HHA
Love in a Puff)

This is a quick-growing climber with dense, feathery foliage, it bears small white flowers which produce highly ornamental and very unusual, inflated seed pods. This vine could also survive some winters but it is easily cut down if it outgrows its welcome.

Cobea (Cathedral Bells, HHA
Cup and Saucer Plant)

Depending on the season, this Mexican climber will grow between I0–20ft (300–600cm) and bears gorgeous bell blooms which have prominent and curled stamens. The variety *C. scandens* bears deep blue flowers and there is a white form, *C. alba*, whose flowers are tinged with green.

Eccremocarpus (Chilean Glory Flower)   HHA

This climber is hardy in favoured districts and bears spikes of tubular flowers throughout the summer. It is available in quite a range of colours – *E. Aureaus* is yellow; *E. scaber* is orange; *E. roseus* bears deep pink flowers. There are also two colour mixtures, 'Anglia Hybrids' and 'Tresco', which range from pink and red to yellow and orange. The seed from these plants is usually extremely viable and you will probably find a carpet of self-sown seedlings if you grow one of these climbers.

Gourds   HHA

These extraordinary plants will trail or climb but they will certainly need support if you want them to go upwards and, whilst the foliage is unexceptional, the fruits are fascinating and highly ornamental. Most catalogues list mixtures which describe the shapes of the gourds but the 'Name of the Year Award' goes to one which is called 'Choose Your Weapon Mixed'!

Humulus (Hop)   HP

The species – *H. Lupulus* is native to Britain and home brewers will value this hardy and vigorous climber which could grow 20ft (600cm) in a year. The Japanese hop, *H. japonicus variegatus*, is not completely hardy but its pale green leaves which are splashed with white are rather like the maple in shape.

Ipomoea (Morning Glory)   HHA

The flowers of this climber are the most beautiful that can be imagined and there are some outstanding varieties from which to choose. The blooms are short-lived and the plant has a somewhat delicate constitution which means that it may not be entirely successful in cold districts but the rewards can be so great that it is worth trying in the sunniest and warmest site in the garden. 'Heavenly Blue' is the most famous variety, followed by 'Scarlet O'Hara' but there are a number of mixtures which will produce magnificently coloured flowers.

Lapageria (Chilean Bell Flower)   HHP

Normally given the protection of a cool greenhouse, this exquisite climber may also be grown outdoors in a really sheltered place but it does need covering during severe weather. The truly gorgeous flowers amply repay the extra trouble but the seed is very expensive, may take three months to germinate and should be sown in a lime-free compost. Two species may be grown, the darkest pink *L. rosea* and the almost white, *L. albiflora*.

Mina (Star Glory)   HHA

This genus is not listed by many seedsmen but where it is found, the more correct name of Quamoclit may be used. The species *M. lobata* bears red flower clusters, which later turn to orange, and another *M. coccinea*, which bears scarlet blooms. There is a further species, *M. pennata*, which is known as the Cypress Vine and has feathery, pale green leaves and red, star-like flowers. The latter species is more tender than the others but they all flower throughout the summer in a sunny position.

Passiflora (Passion Flower)   HHP

There are a number of species which can be grown from seed, the hardiest of which is probably *P. edulis* which bears white flowers and purple and white edible fruits. *P. caerulea* will also do quite well outdoors in a sheltered position and this is the one which has the best-known passion flowers. Seed germination is very erratic indeed.

Rhodochiton (Purple Bell Vine)   HHA

Like some of the other climbers in this section, this is a perennial but its Mexican origins betray its tenderness and it should be grown as an annual. It has heart-shaped leaves and the dark purple flowers with their pink calyces are abundant for many weeks. Again, a warm spot is needed together with some means of support.

Sweet peas   HA

Sweet peas are, of course, the most popular of all

the climbers and they are listed in the 'Best of the Rest' chapter.

Thunbergia (Black-Eyed Susan) HHA

A very popular greenhouse subject but one which will perform well outdoors in a reasonable summer, producing a profusion of yellow, orange or white flowers, each with the characteristic black 'eye'.

Tropaeolum (Canary Creeper) HP

The climbing members of the nasturtium family are not often seen but there are two species which are highly rewarding. *T. peregrinum* has interesting leaves as well as unusual-looking, yellow flowers; *T. speciosum*'s common name is Flame Flower and this too has attractive foliage but with red flowers. The Canary Creeper is simply grown from seed but *T. speciosum* seed requires stratification before it will germinate readily. This entails buying seed in the autumn and sowing it in containers so that it can be exposed to winter temperatures. Hopefully, this breaks the dormancy of the seed but the technique is not always successful. However, if you do succeed, the Flame Flower is a hardy climber and can live for many years.

With the exceptions of ipomoea, humulus and thunbergia, the climbers listed above will need sowing very early in the year to give them the best opportunity to flower effectively. In some cases, it will be even better to sow them during the summer and protect the plants from frost in the winter, planting them out in late spring when temperatures are reliably above freezing.

CHAPTER 15

Bedding on Trial and on Show

Naturally, my hope is that this book proves to be helpful to the beginner and experienced gardener alike, and that it should encourage them to make the best use of bedding plants. However good this book may be, there is no substitute for seeing the real thing. Recommendations are one thing, but looking at a tangible proof of beauty and performance is quite another. There are some institutions, organizations and private companies which do comparative trials of bedding plants, but for the consumer, getting the trials' information is not easy and, in many cases, seeing the trial grounds is inconvenient.

GARDENING WHICH

In 1982, the Consumers Association began publishing *Gardening Which* in an attempt to use their independent testing skills in the gardening arena. As with their other consumer activities, they began testing all manner of equipment and services, giving cultivation tips and instigating trials of a whole range of garden plants. Bedding plants have featured in this work and over the years, more than 200 varieties of the most popular types of plant have been put to the test.

A typical trial concentrates on three or four types of bedding plants and the varieties are chosen to represent those which are commonly available from seed. Four growing sites may be used – perhaps London, Fifeshire, Somerset and North Wales – and the plants are grown, often in local authority parks, according to *Which's* instructions.

The performances are checked throughout the season by invited experts who assess the plants for colour impact, duration of flowering, weather- and disease-resistance, and other important characteristics. The sites are chosen to cover the range of British climatic conditions and many of the trials have noted considerable differences in performance on this account. The season's results are collated and then published in the *Which* magazine at a time when it will guide gardeners in their choice of subjects.

I have encountered some criticism of *Which's* organisation and methods but there is widespread acknowledgement that their results are excellent. The magazine has built a fine reputation and many professional gardeners use it to build up a reference library.

I personally hold the publication in high regard and I believe that their trials' information is the most valuable source for domestic gardeners. Perhaps bedding subjects ought to command more attention from *Gardening Which* but this has to be put in the perspective of the huge range of topics covered by their reports. Whether you would consider it worth the annual subscription of £32 depends on your keenness as a gardener because it could be argued that some of the reports are rather narrow in their appeal. However, many branch libraries will have a copy and I suggest that it should be consulted routinely.

FLEUROSELECT

Seed catalogues are most enthusiastic about mentioning the awards which their varieties have won and although I have not seen any acknowledged as a *Which* 'Best Buy', Fleuroselect winners are almost always brought to our attention.

Fleuroselect is a European organisation which was established in 1970 – principally by flower breeders – to put new varieties on trial, protect breeders' rights and to act as a promotional agency for its membership. There are signs that it will become increasingly international because it does have members from Australia, Japan, India and the US and over half of its medal winners have been flower varieties of non-European origin. There are sixteen trial sites in continental Europe and four in Britain and each award-winning plant must perform well in Southern Italy, Finland and many places in between.

The flower varieties are submitted by the breeders but many new introductions are not given the opportunity for testing, sometimes because of the cost involved, or because the breeder is reluctant to delay the launch of his innovation for a year. This means that many exclusive varieties are never submitted to Fleuroselect – even though they may possess outstanding merit. However, even though some of the best bedding plants may never win this award, there is no doubt that those which are honoured are superb varieties.

To get amongst the medals, a variety must possess a lengthy flowering period, weather- and disease-resistence characteristics, flower quality and originality and appeal to the home gardener. These latter two qualities are questionable because they are not a matter for professional judgement and every gardener in the world could have a different opinion. Perhaps this is why Fleuroselect does reach the occasional mystifying decision. For instance, it was many years before the first gold medal was awarded, despite numerous bronzes and a couple of silvers, but the variety which won the premier accolade was a coreopsis. Without being too rude, it is not a flower of great beauty and one which would be overlooked in any mediocre display. Nonetheless, I must repeat my conviction that any plant which is versatile enough to prosper both in Italy and in Finland deserves our admiration for its performance – if not for its charisma.

Displays of the Fleuroselect award winners can be seen by the public in six British gardens:

- Harlow Car Gardens, Harrogate, Yorkshire.
- King's Heath Park, Birmingham.
- RHS Gardens, Wisley, Surrey.
- Sheffield University Botanic Gardens.
- Sir Thomas and Lady Dixon Park, Belfast.
- Unwins Seeds Trial Grounds, Histon, Cambridge.

THE ROYAL HORTICULTURAL SOCIETY

The RHS is the leading horticultural society in the world and has a membership of over 125,000. Members are entitled to special tickets for shows, lectures and demonstrations and free entry to many notable gardens throughout Britain. There is also a free advisory service on gardening problems and a large collection of free seeds at the end of each year. The society is based at Wisley in Surrey and it is in these extensive and beautiful gardens that an immense amount of trialling is undertaken.

The vast range of work covers trees, shrubs, greenhouse plants, herbaceous subjects, vegetables and, of course, bedding plants.

The society is approached by breeders, seed companies and individuals to test various species and varieties. A special committee decides which to accept and whether other varieties should be requested in order to make each trial representative. Again, this means that the trials are not completely comprehensive but, in the context of Wisley's other commitments, bedding plants are regularly grown and assessed. One example serves to illustrate the scale of the operation: in 1987, eleven types of garden flowers were put on trial, comprising an entry of 653 separate varieties. Of these, seventy-eight were marigolds of which eleven received awards of merit and thrity-three were highly commended. This indicates the high standards achieved by modern marigolds and gives some idea of the work involved; my estimate is that, for this section alone, some 2,000 plants were grown from seed.

The trial grounds are open to the general public who pay admission to the gardens at Wisley but the summaries of the trials, which are published each year, are not widely circulated outside the membership of the RHS.

SPRINGFIELDS GARDENS

Advertised as one of Britain's premier show gardens, Springfields' claim is far too modest, since their displays of garden plants are the best I have seen. The gardens were established in 1966 by means of loans and gifts from Lincolnshire bulb growers, together with some grants, and were meant to be a shop window for local produce. Each spring since then, more than a million bulbs have provided a magnificent spectacle and since 1980, Springfields Gardens have held a summer show of bedding plants together with roses, shrubs and trees.

The bedding enterprise is supported by seed companies which offer their wares free of charge but the decisions about which varieties to display are taken by the Springfields' management and the gardens are dependent for income on admission charges to the public. Many newer strains of bedding plants are grown but, although Springfields have their own award scheme, the gardens cannot be described as trial grounds. The major obligation is to provide a show garden for the public and, therefore, it would obviously be unwise to have large scale experimental beds with totally untried varieties. Nonetheless, the Springfields Certificate of Outstanding Performance, known as SCOOP, is one of the most highly prized awards in the garden industry. The certificates are granted to varieties which give

Fig 100 Red and white tulips underlaid with purple pansies (seen here at the Gateshead Garden Festival) – an unusual blend of colours and one which gives a different impression depending on the viewing distance.

outstanding performance over three successive years at the gardens and the aim is to give further recognition to flowers which have already been extensively put to trial in the UK and abroad.

The gardens are a delight from April until at least October and bedding plant enthusiasts can make their own judgements about the 150,000 plants on show and get some ideas from the various colour associations which are used. Springfields would benefit greatly if there were more display area under glass but greenhouses are expensive and perhaps the peak annual attendance of 80,000 visitors does not allow much spare income for capital development. This figure would be very much greater if Spalding were closer to the centres of population but regardless of its situation, the twenty-five acres of Springfields should be visited by garden lovers, wherever they may live.

HARLOW CAR GARDENS

Situated near to Harrogate in Yorkshire, these gardens are run by the Northern Horticultural Society and offer a wide selection of different displays. There are no real specialities, although roses are a major feature, but there is a great deal of year-round interest.

Fleuroselect flower winners are put on trial routinely to assess their suitability for the north of England and the local climate is a stringent test for any plant. The gardens also initiate their own trials of various subjects, including bedding plants. Typically, two species are chosen and in 1988, for instance, thirty-two varieties of impatiens were grown as well as twenty-one different salvias. The subsequent report showed 'impact' rating at ten-day intervals through the summer, based on the quality and quantity of flowers.

WYTHENSHAWE HORTICULTURAL CENTRE

Based in Wythenshawe Park, in South Manchester, the Wythenshawe Horticultural Centre

Fig 101 The whole of this greenhouse, at Wythenshawe Horticultural Centre, is laid out as if it were an outside bedding scheme.

Fig 102 It is always helpful if plants are clearly labelled, as here at the Wythenshawe Horticultural Centre, especially when it is a lesser known subject like Verbena venosa.

has developed during the last decade into a centre of considerable interest. The bedding trials were initiated by the local manager, Harry Anderton, to enable the public to make their own assessment of the plant varieties which are commonly available. The trials do not claim to be comprehensive but their range has increased each year to include today practically all the most popular flowers.

The centre is also noted for a fine herbaceous border, heather gardens and a magnificent show greenhouse which has been planted with a diverse range of bedding subjects. The park boasts a large walled garden and visitors are welcome to view the nursery area which includes a cactus collection, a tropical house and greenhouses which are devoted to bedding production and display material.

THE SEED COMPANIES

Some of the major retail seed companies run their own trial grounds which enable comparisons to be made between their own varieties and those sold by their competitiors; it also gives

Fig 103 Although marigolds only occupy one part of the colour spectrum, it is amazing how many shades of yellow and brown there are in this trial area at Suttons in Devon.

the opportunity to check that their varieties are true to type and suitable for British conditions. Suttons, Thompson and Morgan, and Unwins have extensive grounds where many thousands of plants are grown but, in the past, they have not all been accessible to the public. Thompson and Morgan have expressed the intention to re-shape their trial area and to open it on a perma-nent basis for visitors in the future.

Suttons recently moved from a site where plants were grown for them under contract, to another area which is under direct company management and, whereas the former grounds were only open for one afternoon a week during the summer, the plan is now to encourage visitors throughout the season.

At Unwins, where the public has long been able to visit during the summer, some detail may be of interest. In 1989, they grew 429 different varieties of flowers and 187 varieties of vegetables; of these flowers, 154 were grown under a code number and marked experimental. (These are the newer ones which the company grows alongside established varieties for com-parison purposes, and presumably include many which are sold by the other seed companies.)

The wholesale seed companies who supply the commercial plant growers also operate large trial grounds but I only know of one which can be seen by the gardening public. This belongs to Colegraves who are based near Banbury in Ox-fordshire and they hold an open day each sum-mer. A small admission charge is made and the proceeds are donated to charity.

Fig 104 Petunias are seen here at Suttons' trial grounds.

Fig 105 Concentric arrangement of 'Universal' pansies. Note the consistency of the colours and the uniformity of shades. This photo was taken at the Gateshead Garden Festival.

All the trial grounds run by seed companies are strictly utilitarian and the plants are grown in straight rows in an open field situation. No attempt is made to provide an ornamental show but anyone who enjoys plants will be fascinated to see so much in such variety and keen gardeners will need a camera and notepad.

OTHER PARKS AND GARDENS

Wythenshawe Park in Manchester has been mentioned as one which conducts and shows comparative bedding trials but there may be many others in Britain, of which I am unaware. This kind of work is often undertaken by local initiative and without publicity, and so it would be prudent to enquire with local parks authorities.

Regardless of trials, however, hundreds of parks boast breathtaking bedding displays. Parks' horticulturalists are usually well acquainted with the latest plant introductions and are amongst the first to grow them; they are often pleased to give information to the public.

One eminent garden which has not been mentioned is Kew, the mother of all botanical institutions, which is a joy to visit. It is a centre for research and home to 60,000 species of plants, although the home gardener is not forgotten. Many of Kew's bedding arrangements are inspirational and frequent examples of the more unusual subjects can be found there.

Many of the stately homes' grounds house memorable bedding displays and so too do the distinguished private gardens which are open to the public. Perhaps the grandest spectacles –

albeit temporary — are those at the garden festivals. Liverpool started the sequence, followed by Stoke and Glasgow at two-yearly intervals, whilst Gateshead held the latest in 1990. All proved outstanding horticultural events which received considerable effort and support from the BBPA and many millions of visitors have been able to see state of the art bedding. The next festival is planned for Ebbw Vale in South Wales in 1992.

In concluding this appraisal of the opportunities to see bedding displays, I must voice disappointement that nowhere — apart from the seed companies' trial grounds — can gardeners have access to a comprehensive range of plants for domestic bedding purposes. Furthermore, those trials do not reveal all and since they are sited in Devon, Suffolk and Cambridgeshire, the convenience factor is very low for most of the population. Ideally, the plant industry and the seed companies should support the establishment of two or three demonstration gardens to allow the public to make their own comparative judgements and also to see suggested plant arrangements and colour schemes. Sadly, this prospect is not even on the horizon although some of the principal members of the BBPA and a couple of the major growers, do have ambitions in this direction. It would be a tremendous boon to gardeners and of very great benefit to the whole of the bedding plant industry.

Fig 106   The vast range of petunia colours on show in the Unwin Seeds trial ground at Histon near Cambridge.

THE AWARD WINNERS

Royal Horticultural Society

Some of the RHS award winners have been mentioned in the plant chapters but the extensive nature of the trials and the fact that many of the certificated varieties are no longer available would make a list of doubtful value. There is a selection of some three dozen winning varieties in the BBPA guide book and gardeners who want further details may be able to buy copies of the RHS's extracts from proceedings by writing to them at Vincent Square, London SWI 2PE.

All American Selections

This is another award system for bedding plants which is much older than its European counterpart — started in 1930. Flower varieties entered for the scheme are grown in thirty-six trial grounds in the US and six in Canada. Some British seed catalogues acknowledge the AAS winners, especially Thompson and Morgan because they have a sales operation and offices in North America. The list of winners now exceeds 100 and many of these varieties have been superseded and are no longer grown but for more information, write to All American Selections, 628 Executive Drive, Willowbrook, Illinois 60521.

Winners (1990)
Achillea 'Summer Pastels'
Celosia 'Pink Castle'
Pansy 'Jolly Joker'
Petunia 'Polo Salmon'
Petunia 'Polo Burgundy Star'

Springfields Certificate of Outstanding Performance – SCOOP

Winners (1987)
Begonia semperflorens 'Stara Rose' and 'Stara White'
Geranium 'Sundance Orange', 'Pulsar Red', 'Pulsar Rose', 'Pulsar Salmon'
Marigold 'Solar Orange' and 'Solar Sulphur'
Salvia 'Red Riches'

Winners (1988)
Dreadful weather conditions at Springfields during July and August of this year resulted in only one award winner:
Nicotiana 'Domino' series.

Winners (1989)
Geranium 'Gala Highlight'
Impatiens 'Super Elfin' series
Marigolds 'Nell Gwynn', 'Suzie Wong', 'Mata Hari', 'Boy' series

Fleuroselect

Winners (1987)	
Impatiens 'Starbright'	Bronze Medal

Winners (1988)	
Dahlia 'Sunny Yellow'	Bronze Medal
Alyssum 'Snow Crystals'	Bronze Medal
Verbena 'Showtime Belle', 'Sandy Scarlet'	Bronze Medal

Winners (1989)	
Coreopsis 'Early Sunrise'	Gold Medal
Lobelia 'Compliment Scarlet'	Bronze Medal
Tagetes 'Disco Golden Yellow' 'Disco Orange', 'Espana Mix', 'Orange Jacket'	Bronze Medal
Dianthus 'Telstar Crimson'	Bronze Medal

Winners (1990)	
Pansy 'Jolly Joker'	Gold Medal
Gazania 'Garden Sun'	Gold Medal

Winners (1991)	
Begonia 'Pin Up'	Gold Medal
Cosmos 'Sonata'	Gold Medal
Dianthus 'Colour Magician' 'Raspberry Parfait', 'Strawberry Parfait'	Gold Medal
Eschscholzia 'Dalli'	Gold Medal
Geranium 'Orange Appeal'	Gold Medal
Pansy 'Imperial Gold Princess', 'Padparadja'	Gold Medal

CHAPTER 16

The Packet Seed Trade

After more than a century of comparative stability, the 1980s brought turmoil to British seed companies with many famous names changing ownership and some disappearing, perhaps permanently. In 1984, Sinclair McGill began selling their seed under the J Arthur Bowers name and the parent company, Fisons, took over Bees and Webbs to use their packing facilities. Owing to a poor level of sales, both Fisons and Bowers seeds were withdrawn and Bees and Webbs were sold to Unwins and may never emerge again. In the meantime, Suttons bought the company which owned Carters, Cuthberts and Dobies but trading continued under all those names — Carters selling through retail outlets; Cuthberts remaining the exclusive Woolworth brand and Dobies staying in the mail order business. Hurst, another well-known seedsman, was taken over but a management buy out in 1989 ensured the continuance of the retail sales.

By the end of the decade, the leading sales' position was held by the Suttons group with annual packet sales in the order of thirty five million; second was Unwins with their sister companies of Marshall and Chelsea Choice; and third place was probably held by the newcomer, Mr Fothergill's, which only started trading in 1980.

Gardening Which began publishing in 1982 and started an annual seed-buying guide with test results on seed from all the larger companies — and some of the smaller ones too. These guides continually bemoaned the fact that flower seed, unlike vegetable seed, does not have to comply with any germination standards and the tests showed considerable differences in quality between the various seedsmen. Suttons and Brown

and Co often received favourable mentions and so too did Mr Fothergill's and Unwins but by the time the 1990 catalogues were circulating, Brown's seed was recommended as the 'Best Buy'.

Brown also began listing the number of seeds in each of their packets, following the example which Mr Fothergill's had set; Chelsea Choice and Marshal gave packet contents *or* the

Fig 107 A display of Verbena 'Garden Party' and French marigold 'Aurora Fire'.

minimum number of plants which could be expected *or* the area of garden which would be covered by the resultant plants. Thompson and Morgan listed the number of seeds in those packets which contained less than fifty and other companies gave the information for expensive seed. Most of the seedsmen emphasised their guarantees of quality but Mr Fothergill's took another step forward by giving the reassurance that, given the correct conditions, more than seventy out of every 100 of their seeds should germinate.

The year 1990 was also that in which many catalogues changed their traditional looks. Thompson and Morgan restyled their famous publication and issued two others – one was an abridged version of the main catalogue and the other was a listing of unusual and challenging plants grown from seed. Unwins changed their long-standing format and put a price of £1.25 on the cover but they also produced an alternative, smaller catalogue which was not priced. Suttons retained their usual format but Dobies marked their move from North Wales to Torquay with a complete change of presentation and I thought that their catalogue was the most attractive of 1990.

Of the flower listings, Thompson and Morgan's main publication remained the largest, with over 2,700 different varieties but competing for the title of the most comprehensive catalogue was that produced by Chiltern Seeds which listed more than 3,700 items, although many of these are trees and shrubs. Unlike the Thompson and Morgan publication – which contained a thousand photographs – the Chiltern booklet is not illustrated but is written in a most agreeable style and makes an excellent reference source; it also contains many items which are unusual and even rare.

Johnson's 1990 catalogue, containing over 275 different flowers, was notable for its cultivation hints, and listings of plants under useful headings. Johnson also offered a number of seed collections based on simple design concepts – the Summer Patches collection contained six packets of different subjects which associate well together and the Summer Shades had six separate varieties in various shades of the same colour. There was obviously some cross-pollination between companies because Mr Fothergill's extended their range of collections. It is always helpful to get suggestions for garden schemes and it is worth remembering that seed collections always represent a saving on individual packet prices.

Regardless of the brand loyalties which exist among gardeners, I do believe that everyone should get as many different catalogues as possible because each company tries to list at least a few items which are not sold elsewhere. To a greater or lesser extent, all these publications contain useful information and many of them are beautifully illustrated. Price comparisons across the companies are not possible because only four catalogues give packet contents but even this is not sufficient on its own. Marshal and Chelsea Choice give the essential information about minimum plants per packet and Mr Fothergill's general comment about expected germination results are a useful yardstick but it is annoying that the rest of the retail trade should be lagging behind. If this unsatisfactory situation persists, we must look towards Brussels to introduce fair and reasonable regulations.

It must be appreciated that maximum germination percentages do vary depending on the flower species and variety. In the case of F_1 geraniums, the figure would normally be over ninety per cent but where the seed viability is considerably less, the cost per plant can be quite startling. For their test in 1989, *Gardening Which* bought a variety of mimulus from one seedsman for £1.34 and the packet contained sixty-four viable seeds. The identical variety from another company cost £1.19 and from this packet, just two seeds germinated which gave a comparative price per plant of 2 pence in one case and almost 60 pence in the other. The *Which* test concluded that the average level of germination was sixty-three per cent for flowers and eighty-three per cent for vegetables but this meant that many of the flower packets yielded less that fifty per cent of viable seed.

In general, the breeders who produce the seed sell their varieties to any of the retail and wholesale companies – although there are some exclusive arrangements – and they often give germination guarantees for their fresh seed. It therefore seems unreasonable that gardeners should not have the same reassurance, always assuming that the retail seedsmen buy the best-quality produce. Clearly, this is not always the case and as all the seed companies claim to test all the seed which they sell, we must doubt the quality control of some seedsmen. Your only practical recourse is to complain as strongly and as often as necessary. If you follow the recommended sowing procedures and the results are not up to reasonable expectations, then send the empty packet to the company and ask for a replacement or a refund.

Some of the trade seed catalogues make excellent reference books, often giving precise cultivation details, but you will find that they only list a restricted range of varieties. This is because they concentrate on commercially successful subjects and, in some cases, these seedsmen have exclusive contracts with particular plant breeders. Names like Booker, Clause, Colegrave, Elite and Royal Sluis may not be familiar to amateur growers but these companies provide much of the seed which is used by commercial nurseries and the nation's parks. There is no reason why you should not buy seed from these sources but the snag is that the smallest trade packets will almost certainly contain far too much seed for a normal garden.

As you might guess, the quality of seed in commercial horticulture is much higher than in the retail trade; I am sure that any company which supplied seed with an average germination of sixty-three per cent to nursery and parks growers, would soon go out of business. Better seed ought to cost more money – but it doesn't; an example will illustrate the point. One of the most expensive seeds of 1990 was the F_1 Multibloom geraniums which were offered by one mail order seedsman at six seeds for £1.95 – that is 32½ pence each – whereas 100 seeds from a trade source cost £11.30 – which is less than 12 pence each. Obviously, we expect unit costs to be lower at the hundred rate but should we expect a difference of 200 per cent?

I am dismayed, in terms of cost and quality, about much of the British packet seed industry and I feel that if standards are not raised, there is a risk of dulling the appetite of those who love growing plants from seed. If this should happen, sales will fall, more companies will disappear and the choice for the consumer will be restricted. Sowing failures are a huge disappointment to gardeners and life is too short to waste time and money on inert capsules which remain inert.

Flower Seed Catalogues

– J W Boyce, Bush Pasture, Low Carter Street, Fordham, Ely, Cambridgeshire CB7 5JU

– D T Brown and Co, Station Road, Poulton-le-Fylde, Blackpool FY6 7HX

– Thomas Butcher, 60 Wickham Road, Shirley, Croydon CR9 8AL

– Chelsea Choice, Regal Road, Wisbech, Cambridgeshire PE13 2RF

– Chiltern Seeds, Bortree Stile, Ulverston, Cumbria LA12 7PB

– Samuel Dobie and Son, Broomhill Way, Torquay, Devon TQ2 7QW

– W W Johnson and Son, London Road, Boston, Lincolnshire PE21 8AD

– S E Marshall and Co, Regal Road, Wisbech, Cambridgeshire PE13 2RF

– Mr Fothergill's Seeds, Gazeley Road, Kentford, Newmarket, Suffolk CB8 7QB

– Suttons Seeds, Hele Road, Torquay, Devon TQ2 7QJ

– Thompson and Morgan, London Road, Ipswich, Suffolk IP2 0BA

– Unwins Seeds, Histon, Cambridge, Cambridgeshire CB4 4LE

There is one further catalogue which is produced

Fig 108   Aster 'Pinochio' on trial at the Sheffield Botanic Garden.

by John Chambers and although it does not list bedding plants, it contains a comprehensive range of 'everlasting' flowers, ornamental grasses and wild flowers.

– John Chambers Wild Flower Seeds, 15, Westleigh Road, Barton Seagrave, Kettering, Northamptonshire NN15 5AJ

There is another publication, from Thompson and Morgan, which will be of interest to the serious gardener. It is called *Growing From Seed* and is published four times a year and available on subscription at an annual cost of £6.95. The same title is used for a publication by Mr Fothergill's which costs 95 pence. (All prices correct at the time of writing.)

CHAPTER 17

The Bedding Plant Industry

Statistics are difficult to obtain for this branch of horticulture but it is thought that annual sales are in the order of £60–70 million and expected to continue rising for many years to come. There has been a rapid expansion in the last ten years or so and in the same period, a tremendous amount of change has taken place.

Formerly, the wholesale seed companies supplied seed to thousands of growers who germinated them, raised the plants and then sold them to retail outlets or direct to the public. Now, although the wholesalers still supply seed, the main part of their business is to raise seedlings and small plants which are known as 'plugs' and a large proportion of growers are now using them. This follows the American pattern where more than half the bedding plant production is from plants and annual sales are about three billion plugs.

This specialization of production enables growers to plan very precisely and, after booking a delivery date, they are secure in the knowledge that their plants will be saleable after a predictable period of growing on. Gone are the potential hazards of germination and with the cell-grown plugs, the process of pricking out is easier and quicker. Naturally, this raises the purchasing costs for the growers but the virtual elimination of plant losses and reduction in nursery labour are major compensating factors.

This revolution has been made possible by the use of high technology machinery in the 'bedding factories', some of which operate on a vast scale. Machines are used which can accurately sow a specified number of seeds per tray, regardless of the individual size of the seed. The plug production depends on incredible devices which sow separate seeds into each compartment of the cellular trays and the latest of these horticultural robots can even prick out seedlings, of all types, at a rate of about 500 per minute! All these innovations are hugely expensive but as long as they are kept working, they are cost-efficient and together with the use of carefully selected seed, the result is a standardized and high-quality product.

Unfortunately, the quality progress which has been made in plant production and followed by many growers has not permeated the whole industry. A great deal of bedding is still raised in traditional ways and there is absolutely nothing wrong with this, although some practices do persist to the disadvantage of the buying public. Perhaps the worst of these is the growing of plants in 'community containers'. There is no doubt that better quality is achieved when the plants are raised in individual compartments; the plants benefit from the absence of competition and when it comes to planting them, the gardener is not faced by the damaging task of disentangling a mass of roots.

Plants raised in cellular containers do occupy more greenhouse space, which is unquestionably expensive to heat, and the containers themselves are more costly than conventional trays and boxes. However, I believe that the benefits far outweigh the relatively small increase in price per plant.

119

One of the most frustrating deficiencies of the bedding trade is the improper labelling of plants and, in this case, it may be the small additional cost which deters some growers from using the excellent labels which are now available. Equally irritating is the use of labels that are so vague that they are insulting; on many occasions, I have encountered labels marked French marigold for example, totally ignoring the fact that it could be any one of fifty varieties. Most likely, it would be the oldest variety of French marigolds known, proudly grown for generations by the grower's predecessors. It certainly is not true that all the newer strains of plants are superior to the older ones but, by and large, the later introductions are an improvement.

The growers, however, are not solely to blame; the whole situation is worsened by the lack of discernment on the part of the consumers. This in turn comes back to a lack of information and guidance which brings me to my last moan about the British bedding industry. The lack of suitable information is especially unhelpful for new generations of gardeners and although the BBPA is well aware of the problem, they do not have the resources to combat the prevailing ignorance. It is estimated that there are between 6,000 to 8,000 growers in this country but the membership of the association is barely 150. Presumably, the vast majority of growers are not willing to make a subscription towards promoting their industry simply because at present, and in the recent past, they have never had it so good. This reflects the fact that, for some time, the demand for bedding has hardly been met and has increased at a rate which has required a huge expansion of production capacity.

The BBPA does publish leaflets for distribution at garden centres and other outlets and the association's *Bedding Plant Guide* is a most attractive booklet which I would recommend to all gardeners. It is well illustrated and contains succinct information on the subject, including lists of plants under helpful headings and a selection of award-winning varieties. Such a handsome publication deserves wide circulation and I hope that it is followed by subsequent editions.

An increase in promotional information is needed – although it is not likely to be significant unless the bedding plant association is successful in recruiting more members, thereby enlarging its budget. In the meantime, as in the past, the industry has relied on one company, Colegrave Seeds, for leadership in the promotional field. This company is linked to one of the world's famous plant breeders, Goldsmith of America, and is the exclusive outlet in Britain for their varieties. Naturally, their marketing efforts are deployed on their own behalf but the rub-off effect has been hugely beneficial to the whole of bedding and far from arousing the envy of their competitors, Colegrave's seem to command universal respect and admiration.

At some point, the responsibility will have to be shared by many more growers otherwise the prophets of doom may prove to be correct. The danger comes from Dutch growers whose co-operative efforts are highly efficient – they are to plants what the Japanese are to motor cars. It would be unfortunate if the Dutch made similar inroads into British bedding to those which they have achieved in other areas of horticulture. The bedding growers of the UK would be unwise if they relied on patriotic purchasing for their future.

Lest I give the impression that British bedding is not of the best, I must emphasize that there is an impressive quantity of the highest quality. Many shops and garden centres will only sell the best and my advice to gardeners is to identify these sources of high standards and value for money, and patronize them. Everyone should get as much information as possible about new plant varieties, either from *Gardening Which* or the gardening press, and also develop sufficient expertise to enable recognition of good quality plants. If the plants prove to be inferior, then complain and keep on complaining until satisfaction is achieved. What the consumer buys or refuses to buy will determine the shape of things to come and bedding plants should be treated like all other consumer items.

Fig 109 Impatiens in a greenhouse at Springfields Gardens.

Very occasionally, some of the nation's largest growers of bedding plants hold open days, enabling the public to see what goes on in a 'bedding factory' and nobody who is interested in plants could fail to be impressed. One that I have visited, Four Oaks Nursery, is close to the Jodrell Bank telescope in central Cheshire and the scale of their operation is formidable. They have about an eight per cent share of the bedding plant market and, in a busy week, the output is in the order of eleven million plants. These are produced by means of the mechanisation which I have mentioned from numerous growing rooms and a total of six acres of greenhouses. A visit to this kind of establishment is a memorable experience.

Things to Come

This book will have left the reader with little doubt that my leanings are very much towards raising plants from seed, even though the modern trend is against this method of domestic production. In the near future, it seems likely that seedlings will gain in popularity but, ultimately, plugs will dominate the market for those who do not favour the majority practice of buying ready-to-plant bedding. This is surely because many garden owners do not wish to become gardeners but do want a home environment which is made more beautiful by plants. I am entirely in sympathy with this sentiment and I recognize that for some, cultivation is irksome and other leisure activities hold greater appeal. The only plea I would make to those who have never sown seed, is to at least give it a try because, as with many things, the journey can be as pleasurable as the arrival. There is considerable satisfaction in admiring glorious flowers which have been nurtured since they were specks in a packet.

Indications are that new varieties will continue to be introduced each year, partly because new and successful flowers can bring financial rewards but also because it is in the nature of plant breeders to explore beyond the present frontiers. Exciting innovations will result but it is also inevitable that some of the developments will be indistinguishable from those which went before.

Rather like the fashion houses of Paris and London, the latest creations will be paraded before eager buyers who will then use their marketing skills to tempt the public. The brave new world of bedding may offer designer plants, colour coordinates and made-to-measure displays but I am hopeful that gardeners will be able to resist the commercial onslaught and indulge their own preferences.

Change is a prerequisite of progress but it is important that the future should be determined by the consumer, which is why I hope that a bedding plant club would be well supported. It could provide a valuable link between what the gardener wants and what the industry provides.* As I have said before, information is the key to improvements but at present, the facts are not sufficiently accessible to the public.

The main case for using seed is that choice is expanded to thousands of varieties whereas buying plants limits you to a few dozen. Nevertheless, whether you use bedding plants for display, grow them for pleasure or both, then I sincerely hope that this book will enable you to improve the show or increase the joy of cultivation. May your garden receive the blessing of ample sunshine and adequate rainfall and may it give you immense pride and pleasure.

* The author would be pleased to hear from gardeners who would be interested in joining such a club.

SOWING TABLES

NAME	TYPE	TEMPERATURES °F	(°C)	GERMINATION TIME WEEKS	SOWING DATE	REMARKS
Abelmoschus	**HHA**	70–80	(21–27)	2–4	Mar	Soak seed in warm water for 2 hours before sowing
Abutilon	**HHP**	65–70	(18–21)	3–4	Feb/Mar	
Achillea	**HP**	65–70	(18–21)	4–10	Jan/Feb	Sow in sandy compost
Adonis	**HA**	55–60	(13–16)	1½–2½	Mar	
Ageratum	**HHA**	65–70	(18–21)	1½–2	Mar/Apr	
Agrostemma	**HA**	55–60	(13–16)	1½–2½	Mar	
Alonsoa	**HHA**	60–70	(16–21)	2–3	Mar	
Althaea	**HA**	55–60	(13–16)	1½–2½	Feb	
Alyssum	**HA**	55–65	(13–18)	1½–2	Mar	Lightly cover seed
Alyssum saxatile	**HP**	55–65	(13–18)	2–3	Jun	Do not cover seed
Amaranthus	**HHA**	70–75	(21–24)	2–4	Feb	
Ammi	**HA**	55–60	(13–16)	2–3	Mar	
Anagallis	**HA**	50–60	(10–16)	2–4	Mar	
Anchusa	**HA**	65–75	(18–24)	2–3	Mar	
Anoda	**HHA**	55–65	(13–18)	2–3	Mar	
Antirrhinum	**HHA**	65–75	(18–24)	2–3	Feb	Lightly cover seed
Arabis	**HP**	60–70	(16–21)	2–4	Jun	Barely cover seed
Arctotis	**HHA**	60–70	(16–21)	3–4	Mar	Care with watering
Argemone	**HHA**	55–65	(13–18)	2–4	Mar	
Asarina	**HHA**	65–70	(18–21)	2–3	Feb	Prick out into pots
Asperula	**HA**	50–60	(10–16)	2–3	Mar	
Aster	**HHA**	65–70	(18–21)	1½–2	Mar/Apr	
Atriplex	**HHA**	65–75	(18–24)	2–3	Apr	
Aubretia	**HP**	60–70	(16–21)	2–4	Jun	Do not cover seed
Auricula	**HP**	60–70	(16–21)	3–5	Jun	Must be kept moist
Bartonia	**HA**	55–65	(13–18)	2–3	Mar	
Begonia (tuberous)	**HHP**	65–70	(18–21)	2–3	Dec/Mar	Supplementary light needed if sown before March. Surface sow and maintain maximum humidity
Begonia semperflorens	**HHA**	65–75	(18–24)	2–3	Jan/Feb	Surface sow and maintain maximum humidity
Bellis	**HB**	55–65	(13–18)	2–3	May/Jun	
Brachycome	**HHA**	65–80	(18–27)	2–4	Mar	Barely cover seed
Brassica	**HA**	50–60	(10–16)	1½–3	Mar/Apr	
Bupleurum	**HP**	50–60	(10–16)	2–3	Mar	
Calandrinia	**HHA**	55–60	(13–16)	2–2½	Mar	
Calceolaria	**HHA**	60–70	(16–21)	2–3	Feb	
Calendula	**HA**	55–65	(13–18)	1½–3	Apr	
Campsis	**HHA**	70–75	(21–24)	4–12	Dec/Jan	Do not cover seed
Candytuft	**HP**	65–75	(18–24)	1½–4	May/Jun	Often erratic germination
Canna	**HHP**	70–80	(21–27)	3–10	Jan/Feb	Soak seed for 24 hours. Often erratic germination

SOWING TABLES

NAME	TYPE	TEMPERATURES °F	(°C)	GERMINATION TIME WEEKS	SOWING DATE	REMARKS
Cardiospermum	**HHA**	70–80	(21–27)	3–5	Jan	
Carnation	**HP**	60–70	(16–21)	1½–2½	Feb	
Carthamus	**HA**	55–65	(13–18)	2–3	Mar	
Celosia	**HHA**	65–80	(18–27)	1½–3	Mar/Apr	Ensure compost is moist
Centaurea	**HA**	60–75	(16–24)	1–2½	Mar	
Centaurium	**HA**	55–70	(13–21)	2–3	Mar	
Cerastium	**HP**	55–70	(13–21)	1½–3	Mar/Apr	
Chrysanthemum	**HA**	60–70	(16–21)	2–3	Feb/Mar	
Cineraria maritima	**HHA**	65–75	(18–24)	2–3	Feb/Mar	
Clarkia	**HA**	60–75	(16–24)	1½–3	Apr	
Clary	**HP**	55–70	(13–21)	2–4	Mar	
Cleome	**HA**	50–65	(10–18)	2–3	Mar/Apr	Do not cover seed
Coleus	**HHP**	65–80	(18–27)	2½–4	Apr	
Collinsia	**HA**	55–75	(13–24)	1½–3	Mar	
Convolvulus	**HA**	65–80	(18–27)	2–3	Mar	Soak seed for two hours
Cordyline	**HHP**	65–80	(18–27)	3–6	Jan/Feb	Soak seed for 24 hours. Erratic germination
Coreopsis	**HP**	60–70	(16–21)	2–4	Jan/Feb	
Cosmos	**HHA**	60–75	(16–24)	1½–2	Mar	
Craspedia	**HHA**	65–75	(18–24)	2–3	Mar	
Crepis	**HA**	65–80	(18–27)	2–3	Mar	
Cuphea	**HHP**	65–80	(18–27)	3–4	Feb/Mar	Barely cover seed
Dahlia	**HHP**	65–75	(18–24)	1½–2½	Apr	Grows quickly in warmth
Delphinium	**HA**	55–65	(13–18)	1½–2	Mar	Do not exceed 65°F (18°C)
Delphinium	**HP**	55–65	(13–18)	2–4	Jan	Sometimes erratic
Dimorphotheca	**HHA**	60–70	(16–21)	2–3	Mar/Apr	Barely cover seed
Eccremocarpus	**HHA**	65–70	(18–21)	4–10	Dec/Jan	Barely cover seed
Echium	**HA**	55–65	(13–18)	2–3	Mar/Apr	
Eryngium	**HP**	65–70	(18–21)	1–10	Jan/Feb	Surface sow. Chilling may be necessary before sowing
Eschscholzia	**HA**	60–70	(16–21)	2–4	Mar	
Eucalyptus	**HHP**	70–80	(21–27)	2–12	Dec/Jan	
Euphorbia	**HHA,HP**	70–75	(21–24)	3–4	Feb/Mar	
Gaillardia	**HHA**	65–70	(18–21	2–4	Feb/Mar	Do not cover seed
Gazania	**HHA**	65–80	(18–27)	2–3	Mar/Apr	
Geranium	**HHP**	70–75	(21–24)	1–1½	Jan	
Glaucium	**HA**	60–65	(16–18)	2–3	Mar	
Godetia	**HA**	60–70	(16–21)	1–2	Mar/Apr	
Gomphrena	**HHA**	60–75	(16–24)	2–3	Mar	
Gourds	**HHA**	75–80	(24–27)	2–4	Mar	Soak seed for 48 hours before sowing
Grasses	**HA**	55–70	(13–21)	2–3	Apr	Lightly cover seed
Gypsophila	**HA,HP**	60–70	(16–21)	2–3	Mar	Some perennials will flower first year from a January sowing
Helianthus	**HA**	65–80	(18–27)	1–2	Apr	
Helichrysum	**HHA**	65–80	(18–27)	1–2	Apr	Barely cover seed
Heliotrope	**HHA**	65–80	(18–27)	1–3	Mar/Apr	Slightly erratic
Herbs	**HA,HP**	55–70	(13–21)	1–4	Feb/Mar	
Hibiscus	**HHP**	60–75	(16–24)	2–3	Feb/Mar	

SOWING TABLES

NAME	TYPE	TEMPERATURES °F	(°C)	GERMINATION TIME WEEKS	SOWING DATE	REMARKS
Humulus	**HP**	55–70	(13–21)	2–3	Feb/Mar	
Hypoestes	**HHA**	65–80	(18–27)	1½–2	Mar/Apr	
Impatiens	**HHA**	70–75	(21–24)	2–3	Mar/Apr	Germinate in good light and high humidity
Ipomoea	**HHA**	70–80	(21–27)	1–3	Mar	Soak or chip seed before sowing
Kochia	**HHA**	65–75	(18–24)	1½–2	Apr	Surface sow
Lantana	**HHP**	65–80	(18–27)	4–10	Jan/Feb	Soak seed for 24 hours. Erratic germination
Lapageria	**HHA**	60–75	(16–24)	4–10	Jan	Soak seed for 2 hours. Use lime-free compost. Keep dark
Lavatera	**HA**	60–70	(16–21)	2–3	Mar	
Layia	**HA**	60–70	(16–21)	1½–3	Mar	
Leptosiphon	**HA**	55–65	(13–18)	2–3	Mar	
Limnanthes	**HA**	55-65	(13–18)	2–3	Mar	
Limonium	**HHA**	65–75	(18–24)	1½–3	Mar	
Linaria	**HA**	55–70	(13–21)	2–3	Mar	Lightly cover seed
Linum	**HA**	60–70	(16–21)	2–3	Mar	
Lobelia	**HHA**	65–80	(18–27)	1½–3	Feb	Surface sow
Lonas	**HA**	60–70	(16–21)	1–2	Mar/Apr	
Lupin	**HA**	60–70	(16–21)	3–4	Mar	Sometimes erratic
Malope	**HA**	65–70	(18–21)	2–3	Mar/Apr	
Marigold	**HHA**	65–75	(18–24)	1–1½	Apr	
Matricaria	**HHA**	65–70	(18–21)	2–3		Surface sow
Matthiola	**HB,HHA**	55–70	(13–21)	1–2	Mar	Sow biennials in summer
Mesembryanthemum	**HHA**	65–70	(18–21)	2–3	Mar	Surface sow and germinate in darkness
Mimulus	**HHA**	65–70	(18–21)	2–3	Mar	Surface sow. Keep moist
Mina	**HHA**	65–75	(18–24)	4–6	Jan/Feb	Sow in individual pots
Molucella	**HHA**	65–80	(18–27)	2–3	Mar	Lightly cover seeds. Erratic
Myosotis	**HB**	65–70	(18–21)	2–3	June/July	Barely cover seeds
Nasturtium	**HA**	60–70	(16–21)	1½–3	Apr	
Nemesia	**HHA**	55–65	(13–18)	1½–3	Mar	Surface sow
Nemophila	**HA**	55–65	(13–18)	2–3	Mar	Do not exceed 65°F (18°C)
Nicotiana	**HHA**	65–80	(18–27)	1½–3	Mar/Apr	Barely cover seeds
Nigella	**HA**	66–75	(18–24)	1–2	Mar/Apr	Keep moist
Nolana	**HHA**	65–80	(18–27)	2–3	Mar	
Oenothera	**HHA**	65–80	(18–27)	2–4	Mar	
Pansy	**HP**	65–75	(18–24)	2–3	Mar	Sow summer for spring flowers
Passiflora	**HHP**	65–80	(18–27)	6–12	Dec/Jan	Soak seed for 24 hours
Penstemon	**HHA**	70–80	(21–27)	2–5	Feb/Mar	
Petunia	**HHA**	70–80	(21–27)	2–3	Mar/Apr	Surface sow
Phacelia	**HA**	55–70	(13–21)	2–3	Mar	
Phlox	**HHA**	60–70	(16–21)	2–3	Mar	
Polyanthus & Primula	**HP**	55–65	(13–18)	3–5	May/Jun	Surface sow. Keep below 65°F (18°C)
Polygonum	**HHA**	65–75	(18–24)	2–4	Feb/Mar	
Poppy	**HA**	55–65	(13–18)	2–3	Mar/Apr	

SOWING TABLES

NAME	TYPE	GERMINATION TEMPERATURES °F	(°C)	TIME WEEKS	SOWING DATE	REMARKS
Portulaca	**HHA**	70–80	(21–27)	2–3	Mar	Lightly cover seeds
Pyrethrum	**HHA**	55–65	(13–18)	3–5	Feb/Mar	Sometimes erratic
Reseda	**HA**	60–70	(16–21)	2–3	Mar/Apr	
Rhodochiton	**HHA**	60–70	(16–21)	2–6	Jan/Feb	Erratic germination
Ricinus	**HHP**	65–75	(18–24)	1–2	Apr	
Rudbeckia	**HHA**	70–80	(21–27)	1½–3	Mar/Apr	Lightly cover seed
Salpiglossis	**HHA**	65–80	(18–27)	2–4	Mar	Barely cover seed
Salvia	**HHA**	65–75	(18–24)	1–2	Apr	Lightly cover seed
Sanvitalia	**HHA**	65–75	(18–24)	1–2	Mar	Barely cover seed
Scabiosa	**HA**	60–75	(16–24)	1–3	Apr	
Schizanthus	**HHA**	60–70	(16–21)	2–3	Mar/Apr	Barely cover seed
Silene	**HP**	55–70	(13–21)	2–3	Jan/Feb	
Sweet Pea	**HA**	55–65	(13–18)	2–3	Feb/Mar	Chip those seeds which do not germinate
Swiss Chard	**HA**	55–65	(13–18)	1–3	Mar	
Tagetes	**HHA**	65–75	(18–24)	1–2	Apr	
Thunbergia	**HHA**	65–75	(18–24)	2–3	Mar	
Thymophylla	**HHA**	60–75	(16–24)	2–3	Mar	
Tithonia	**HHA**	70–80	(21–27)	2–3	Apr	
Tropaeolum peregrinum	**HA**	60–75	(16–24)	2–4	Feb/Mar	
Tropaeolum speciosum	**HP**	60–75	(16–24)	4–10	Dec/Jan	Seed needs chilling before warm sowing
Urinia	**HHA**	55–70	(13–21)	2–3	Mar	Barely cover seed
Venidium	**HHA**	60–70	(16–21)	1–2	Apr	
Verbena	**HHA**	70–80	(21–27)	1½–3	Mar/Apr	Slightly erratic. Keep compost fairly dry
Vinca	**HHA**	65–75	(18–24)	2–3	Mar	
Viola	**HP**	65–75	(18–24)	2–3	Feb/Mar	
Viscaria	**HA**	55–70	(13–21)	2–3	Mar	
Wallflower	**HB**	65–75	(18–24)	1–2	Jun/Jul	
Xeranthemum	**HA**	55–70	(13–21)	1–2	Mar	
Zea	**HHA**	65–75	(18–24)	1–2	Apr	Better sown in individual pots
Zinnia	**HHA**	65–75	(18–24)	1–2	April	

Notes to the seed sowing tables

The temperature range in the tables is that which will give optimum germination results but most seed will germinate outside the range given although the results will usually be slower and more erratic. The temperatures listed should be that of the compost in which the seed is sown.

Pre-soaking in warm water is beneficial for some hard-coated seeds. Those which show signs of swelling should be sown; those which do not can be chipped with a file. The purpose is to damage the hard seed coat so that moisture can penetrate.

Most seed will germinate satisfactorily in the light or the dark but where the table remarks recommend surface sowing or only a light covering of compost, this indicates that germination will be much better in a light position – but not in direct sunshine.

High humidity, when it is required, can be easily achieved by placing the seed pan or pot in a plastic bag.

The time taken for seedlings to emerge can be variable, especially if the preferred temperature range is not maintained.

The recommended sowing dates are intended as a guide for an 'average' year in which the late frosts finish by the end of May.

All the hardy annuals (**HA**) can be sown outdoors, in the ground or in containers, from the end of March onwards; the hardy perennials (**HP**) can be sown outdoors in the summer.

Index